The $100,000 Decision

Other McGraw-Hill books by Robert Irwin:

HOW TO BUY A HOME AT A REASONABLE PRICE
HOW TO BUY AND SELL REAL ESTATE FOR FINANCIAL SECURITY
PROTECT YOURSELF IN REAL ESTATE (with Richard Brickman)
RICHES IN REAL ESTATE
THE REAL ESTATE AGENT'S AND INVESTOR'S TAX BOOK (with Richard
Brickman)

About the Author

*Robert Irwin was a successful real estate broker for years and helped
many a buyer and seller get through difficult real estate transactions.
Later he became a successful private investor himself.*

He is the former editor of two newsletters received by brokers—
Real Estate Age *and* Real Estate Update *and for the past 18 years
has held a California broker's license. In addition to numerous
articles, Robert Irwin is the author of seven popular books on
technical and investment aspects of real estate.*

ROBERT IRWIN

The $100,000 Decision

*The Older American's Guide to Selling
a Home and Choosing Retirement Housing*

McGRAW-HILL BOOK COMPANY

*New York   St. Louis   San Francisco   Auckland   Bogotá   Hamburg
Johannesburg   London   Madrid   Mexico   Montreal   New Delhi   Panama
Paris   São Paulo   Singapore   Sydney   Tokyo   Toronto*

333.33
I7280
c-1
14.95
6/81

Library of Congress Cataloging in Publication Data

Irwin, Robert
   The $100,000 decision.

      1. House selling—United States.   2. Aged—
   United States–Dwellings.   I. Title.
   HD1379.I655   333.33′3   80-28974

ISBN 0-07-032070-5

1 2 3 4 5 6 7 8 9 0   DODO   8 9 8 7 6 5 4 3 2 1

The editors for this book were William Newton and Virginia F. Blair, the designer was
Elliot Epstein, and the production supervisor was Sally Fliess. It was set in Souvenir light
by David E. Seham Incorporated.

Printed and bound by R. R. Donnelly & Sons Company.

For Mo and Marion

CONTENTS

PREFACE

Just a few years ago if you tried to take the money out of your house to retire on, you might end up paying a large portion of it in taxes to Uncle Sam. If your gain was $100,000, you might pay $25,000, $30,000, or more in taxes depending on how long you had owned the property, your tax bracket, and other factors.

Losing a quarter or more of your gain to taxes was a terrible blow. Statistics indicate that most people chose not to sell, rather than to take the loss. Often that meant that they were stuck in a house that didn't suit their retirement needs, and they didn't have the cash they needed for retirement.

Today, it's different. Today it's possible to cash in that house, get up to $100,000 in gain, and *not pay a cent in taxes* on it to the federal government. Today, it's no longer a matter of being forced to keep your house out of fear of heavy taxation. Today, it's a matter of deciding whether or not to go for the $100,000 exclusion.

Most people have heard of this relatively new law, the $100,000 exclusion, but, they're not quite sure what it is, when to take it, who qualifies, and so on. Even the information passed out by the Internal Revenue Service supposedly explaining the rule is complex and difficult to understand.

That's where this book comes in. Its purpose is to explain the $100,000 exclusion in easy-to-read language so you can quickly understand it. It will show you whether you qualify, how much you'll get, and what your housing options at retirement really are.

This book is for the person who wants to know about this new law. It's also for the individual who wants to know what kind of hous-

ing is best suited to retirement needs. Housing alternatives are extensively discussed. And it's also for people who are wondering how to
invest and protect from inflation their retirement dollars, including the
money from the up to $100,000 exclusion, should they get it.

This book can be a valuable supplement to preretirement planning
and counseling. It can show you how to save big money in taxes. Most
important, it can aid you in making the right financial and housing
decisions at one of the most crucial times of your life.

The $100,000 Decision

INTRODUCTION: THE $100,000 DECISION WILL CHANGE THE REST OF YOUR LIFE

A few years ago Congress passed a law that has become known as the "$100,000 decision." It has helped thousands of people cash in their homes and get *tax-free* dollars to retire on. At the same time, because of confusion surrounding it, it has caused great disappointment and some financial hardship for those who suddenly discovered they didn't qualify, and many have been surprised and concerned that they didn't get as much as they thought they would.

The new law was regarded as a $100,000 gift by many, but it was a gift with dozens of strings attached. In general the law says that people who reach the age of 55 can, *once in their lifetime,* exclude (meaning not pay) federal income taxes on gain from the sale of their home, up to $100,000. But what if you're 55 and your husband or wife isn't: Do you still qualify? What happens when there's a divorce? Or death? What about someone who has already taken the up to $35,000 exclusion that was formerly on the books: Does he or she qualify for a second exclusion? What if you're single: Do you get up to the full $100,000 or only half? Do you have to live in the house to qualify? How long must you have lived there? If you do qualify, how do you actually get the money? (These and many more questions are answered in Chapters 1 and 2.)

Just knowing that there is an up to $100,000 exclusion out there isn't the same as getting it. It also is not the same as knowing when to take it or even whether you should go for it at all. The $100,000 decision in reality is only one factor in the context of overall retirement plans. What sort of a retirement home you will want if you get the exclusion and how much your new home will cost are equally important considerations.

Everyone who's nearing 55 (some much sooner, others later) begins wondering where and in what kind of style they are going to spend their retirement years. Of course, we all want it to be a time of relaxation and leisure, but what's really practical and possible? A cabin near a stream in the mountains may sound ideal to the spouse who loves fishing, but it may be a lot less than desirable to the other spouse who happens to be worried about shopping, cooking, and washing miles from stores, friends, and electricity.

Perhaps a retirement village in sunny Florida or Arizona would be ideal. What about just moving to a smaller house, or a condominium, or a mobile home, or even an apartment? For those with medical problems, is a retirement hotel or other care facility a real alternative? These are all possibilities and they all have their advantages, but they also have important drawbacks which should be considered. (Housing alternatives are discussed in detail in Chapters 3 to 9.)

For most people retirement is not easy. It involves certain common problems including difficulty in structuring a nonworking day, dealing with a potential loss of prestige, and sometimes, overcoming marital friction. These are psychological concerns that nearly everyone faces sooner or later.

I can't help with these psychological concerns (in some cases personal counseling can be very useful), but by giving you sound options in terms of saving tax dollars, finding suitable housing, and making wise financial decisions, I can give you time and opportunity to work on these retirement transition difficulties. If you're not worried about where you're going to live or where your next dollar is coming from, you have much more energy for dealing with the psychological concerns of retirement.

You can make the $100,000 decision only once in your lifetime. If you make it poorly, you may live to regret it every day of the rest of your life, but if you make it wisely, you will find your life filled with the satisfaction that comes from knowing you have a secure home and are on the way to financial independence.

ONE

How to Get the Up to $100,000 Exclusion

The up to $100,000 exclusion may be the single biggest tax break the federal government has ever given to the near-retirement taxpayer. But, what exactly is the exclusion? How do you qualify for it? How do you get it?

Perhaps the best way to answer these questions is to take an example of a couple who did get the exclusion, Marge and Peter Howard. They saw their retirement dreams realized by taking advantage of what the government offered.

Peter worked for a large corporation. Marge had been a clothes buyer for a department store for some 15 years at one point but had retired from business and become a homemaker 10 years before the couple decided to take the $100,000 exclusion. Peter was 59 years old, Marge 58.

Peter's company offered a preretirement seminar for employees who reached age 59. The seminar was intended to give mature employees a picture of what they could expect at least 5 years before their intended retirement time, so they would have ample opportunity to make important financial decisions before they left work. Both Peter and Marge attended the company seminar, which lasted an entire day. The company paid for the speakers and for a complimentary lunch.

Before going, Marge said to Peter, "They're probably going to tell you that your retirement plan was a big mistake and you'll just get a gold watch." Peter did not think the joke was in good taste and assured Marge that the company retirement plan was sound. It was.

At the meeting, a company representative explained the general terms of the retirement package. Each employee had so much money coming on the basis of length of employment. The vesting period for the company was 15 years. That meant that you had to work for the full 15 years in order to receive all the money in your account. If you had worked less than 15 years at the time of retirement, then only a portion of the money accumulated in the account would be turned over. If you had only worked 10 years, for example, then you'd only get two-thirds. Since Peter had worked for more than 15 years, he was entitled to all the money in his retirement account.

Near the end of the day, the seminar broke up into small groups, and each employee's exact pension was calculated. Peter found out he could either take his money out all at once or, if he wanted, receive it over a period of years. If he elected to receive it for 20 years, he would get $623 per month.

In addition, the company spokesman also told the Howards how much they could expect each from social security. Before the small groups broke up, Peter and Marge knew exactly how much money they could expect to receive during their retirement years whether they chose to wait until Peter was 65, or took an earlier retirement. (If you do not have access to such a company-sponsored meeting, you would be wise to check with your accounting department to see exactly what to expect from your retirement pension.)

Just before closing the seminar, the speaker said, "There are a few other things I want to mention. One of them is the new $100,000 exclusion the government is allowing people over 55 years of age on their house. This may be of benefit to you in that it is a way to get a sizable amount of cash, tax-free. I suggest you talk to a real estate broker to find out how much money you have in your property."

Both Peter and Marge were enthused about the idea of getting money tax-free and raised their hands to get more information. However, the meeting was already over. After the meeting they talked with the group leader, Karen, who told them she really didn't know much more than she had already said about the house exclusion.

Marge and Peter decided that knowing how much they could expect each month really was only half of their retirement financial concerns. The other half was how much money they would have available in cash both to buy another home, if they so desired, and as a reserve against emergencies such as accidents or illness. Their cash position was vitally important to them.

They wanted to learn more about the $100,000 exclusion. Marge and Peter had bought their home from a real estate broker named Leon. They decided to contact him and find out exactly what they could hope to get.

Leon had, by then, himself retired, but he kept up with the market and agreed to tell them what he knew. He said he wouldn't advise them, but would just throw out some ideas about what could be done. He pointed out that since each person's tax situation was totally different and since he really didn't know about theirs, they shouldn't rely just on what he said. They should check with a certified public accountant (CPA) or an attorney before making any decisions. (You, the reader, should also not rely on Leon's explanation, but should check with your CPA or attorney before taking any action on the $100,000 exclusion.)

Leon explained that the most important thing they should understand about the exclusion was that it was not a gift of money to them from the government. "The government isn't going to send you a check for a certain amount of money just because you reached the age of 55," he said.

"To put it most simply, you have to own a home," he continued. "The way it works is that in order to get the money, you have to sell your house. Then, if you qualify (see Chapter 2), up to $100,000 of the *gain* you receive from the sale will not be taxed. Any money you get is from the sale of your home. What you save is the cash you would otherwise have to pay in taxes on that money from the house."

"Do you mean," Marge said, "that there isn't an automatic $100,000?"

"That's correct," Leo said. "This is an *up to* $100,000 exclusion. If it turns out you only have a gain upon the sale of your home of $25,000, then you'd only get that much excluded (not taxed). On the other hand, if you had a gain of $175,000, then only the first $100,000 would be tax-free." (The other $75,000 might also not be immediately taxed under certain conditions; see Chapter 2.)

"What we need to know, then," Peter offered, "is how much money we're going to get."

"Yes," Leon said. "It will be helpful to you to know that. But the government doesn't really calculate taxes on how much cash you get.

It's interested in something called 'gain.' I think you can understand gain if you first understand 'equity.' Your equity is your interest in the property, or how much money you would actually get out if you sold right away."

CALCULATING THE EQUITY

Leon questioned them about how much money they owed on their house. Marge had brought their last loan statement along and said it came to $37,417. "That's the current outstanding balance on our mortgage."

Then Leon asked if they had any other mortgages or liens against their property. (A lien is a money encumbrance. It ties up the title and you normally can't sell until it's paid off. Frequently liens are put on property when the owners borrow money and fail to repay. Most people do not have unknown liens on their homes.) Peter said they didn't.

Leon then calculated the amount of their equity (the value of their interest in their home). He said their equity was equal to the difference between what they owed on the property and the amount they could sell it for, less costs of sale.

DETERMINING THE COSTS OF SALE

Real Estate Commission

"I know your house, since I sold it to you," Leon said. "I believe it would get about $145,000 on today's market. Of course, there would be the costs of sale. We'll figure the real estate commission at 5 percent. [Note: Real estate commissions are arbitrary; there is no set or fixed rate. The commission to be paid is agreed upon between seller and agent.] Then we can quickly see what your commission cost will be."

$$\begin{array}{r} \$145,000 \\ \times \quad .05 \\ \hline \$ \quad 7,250.00 \end{array}$$

"It's going to cost you about $7,000 in broker's fees alone to sell your home. Of course, you could try to sell without a broker, but having been in the business for many years," Leon said, "I've seen very few people successfully sell 'by owner.' Most buyers are simply shy of dealing directly with the owner. They like the distance that having an agent puts between them and the seller. While they might hesitate to offer less directly to a seller's face, they don't hesitate for an instant to have their agent make a lower offer. My advice has always been to try and sell it yourself for a few weeks. Then, if it doesn't work out, get yourself a good agent."

Closing Costs

Leon pointed out that in addition to the real estate broker's commission, there were also other "closing" or sales costs. These included fees for title insurance, attorneys, document recordation, document preparation, and termite clearance. He said any good title insurance company could estimate these fees very quickly for them. Finally, there were "prorations." These were costs that they might have when such things as taxes, insurance, or utility expenses were split between buyer and seller.

"Those are the ongoing costs of ownership," he said. "For example, if you've already paid a year's worth of taxes in advance, yet sell only six months into the tax year, you would expect the buyer to compensate you for half of the taxes. This would be 'prorating' them. On the other hand, if you hadn't yet paid the taxes and we were halfway into the year, you might expect to pay the buyer compensation for the six months you had owned the property. The result of prorations may be either that you receive money or that you pay it out."

Peter nodded that he understood about closing costs and prorations. He asked Leon to get on with the $100,000 exclusion. Marge said to let Leon take his time. He didn't know how much they knew and he was just going one step at a time to be sure they understood perfectly.

Leon said, "We'll guess that your closing costs are $2,000 in addition to the commission. Now we can determine how much equity you have."

Sales price	$145,000	
Less commission	7,250	
Less closing costs	2,000	
Total after costs	$135,750	$135,750
Less amount to pay off old mortgage*		37,750
		$ 98,000

*There was a penalty of $333 for paying off this loan early.

"You have an equity of about $98,000," Leon said. "That's how much you can expect out of your house if you sell for cash." (In this context, "cash sale" means getting all the seller's money out, not leaving some in the property in the form of a second mortgage, contract of sale, or other such device.)

Marge interrupted, "So, what you're saying is that we'll get $98,000 tax-free, since the exclusion is *up to* $100,000."

Leon said that was not at all what he meant to say. Thus far they had been calculating *equity,* or the seller's interest in the property. Equity, however, is not what the exclusion is based upon. The government calculates in a way that is much different. It is concerned with something called "gain."

Both Peter and Marge looked puzzled. Finally Peter said, "Do you mean that the money we get out upon the sale is not what the tax is based on?"

"Yes, it often works that way," Leon replied.

"I know what equity is," Marge continued, "but I guess I just don't understand what you mean by 'gain'."

"It's not that hard," Leon said. He pointed out that the federal government looks upon the purchase of a house basically as an investment. He noted that if it were the principal residence, certain specific rules would apply (see Chapter 2), but nonetheless calculations were made when figuring taxes as if it were a piece of investment property. In order to figure gain, they first had to know about things such as "basis" and "adjusted sales price."

"The first thing we should get clear," Leon said, "is what 'basis' is."

BASIS

Marge and Peter looked at Leon and waited. They had heard their accountant mention basis, but had never really understood the term.

"Basis," Leon continued, "in the case of most personal homes (although not always) is what it costs you for the property, plus or minus certain other terms. We'll say it's the amount of your initial investment."

"What you're saying then," Peter commented, "is that this basis thing is in reality just the price we paid for the house."

"Essentially that's true," Leon replied. (Of course there are always exceptions—for example, when you build, in which case the cost of construction might help to determine your basis.) "And," Leon continued, "there are certain plus or minus costs. For example, usually all escrow and filing fees, legal services connected with the sale, legal services connected with the title policy, and sometimes 'points' are *added* to the purchase price."

"Why added?" Marge asked. "I should think they would be subtracted."

Leon smiled and pointed out that they were costs that the buyer was paying in addition to the sales price. Therefore, in reality they actually did raise the cost of the house.

"Before we go on," Peter interrupted, "there's a term you used that puzzles me. What are 'points'?"

Points

Leon explained that usually when a new loan is obtained by a buyer, the lender charges a certain number of points depending on the money market conditions. A point is equal to 1 percent of the loan amount. One point for a loan of $10,000 would be $100. Leon said that in some cases, these points constitute a one-time fee which includes the appraisal, legal, and processing costs. If that's the case, then the points normally can be added to the cost of purchase. On the other hand, he noted that sometimes the points were in reality prepaid interest.

"Once we know what you paid for the property and your costs of purchase, we can find out your original basis."

Peter had brought a bag full of documents along just in case they would be needed. He fished through them and finally found their original closing statement from when they purchased their home. They spread it out on Leon's table and examined it, adding up all the appropriate fees. (Note: The distribution of actual fees—whether they add to the purchase price or subtract from it when calculating basis—is a technical area best left to accountants.)

Original purchase price	$20,000
Fees which Leon thought could be added	
	1,000
Basis of property	$21,000

"$21,000," Leon commented, "is the *basis* of your property. It's the amount from which we start, your initial investment."

Peter interrupted, "What you're saying, then, is that instead of our remaining loan balance, we subtract our *basis* from the sales price of $145,000, and that gives us our gain."

"Not quite," Leon continued. "What we have here is your basis in the property. What we need is your *adjusted* basis."

ADJUSTED BASIS

Peter and Marge looked at each other. Finally Marge said, "Is adjusted basis different from just plain old basis?"

Leon smiled and said that frequently it was. "The government says you must increase your basis for improvements, additions, and other capital items. It also says you must reduce your basis for losses from fire (or other casualty losses), any payments you receive for any easements or rights-of-way, and of course, for any 'depreciation.' But, since this is your personal residence and you don't have a business use for it, it doesn't have any depreciation."

"Does that mean," Marge said, "that if we lose part of the house because of a fire, we must reduce the original basis?"

"Yes, it does," Leon said. "And then you must increase it if and when you rebuild."

"For example," Peter interjected, "if we had built a swimming pool?"

Basis	$21,000
Pool	10,000
Adjusted basis	$31,000

"That qualifies as an addition," Leon noted and said if they had paid $10,000 for the pool and kept all the bills and so had evidence of the costs of work done, they could add it to the basis.

"In any event, we didn't add a pool, so our *adjusted* basis is $21,000. Can we now subtract the *adjusted basis* from the sales price?" Peter asked.

"Almost," Leon continued. "We first have to find what your *adjusted* sales price is."

ADJUSTED SALES PRICE

Peter and Marge again looked at each other. This time Marge said, "I presume the adjusted sales price is what we get for the house less the costs of sale?"

"Exactly," said Leon. "It's really quite simple. We'll assume you receive $145,000 as your sales price. From this we'll subtract the full commission you have to pay; your escrow, filing, and legal fees; and many other fees involved with the sale. You'll of course have to check with your accountant to see just what fees you must add or subtract from the sales price in your particular case. We'll assume that all the allowable fees come to $9,000."

Sales price	$145,000
Less sales costs	9,000
Adjusted sales price	$136,000

"Now," Peter said, "can we at last find out what our real profit from the sale of the house is?"

Leon didn't hear what Peter had said because he was making the calculation.

Adjusted sales price	$136,000
Less adjusted basis	21,000
Gain on sale	$115,000

"The amount of your gain on sale would be $115,000," Leon announced.

"That can't be right," Marge said. "Just a moment ago you pointed out that we'd only be receiving out $98,000 in cash as our equity in the house. Now you're saying that we're going to be taxed on $115,000. How can we be taxed on more than we make? You must have made a mistake in your calculations."

EQUITY

Leon sat back in his chair and looked thoughtful. Finally he said, "I think the problem here comes about because you're confusing gain with equity. If you ask most people what they have in their house, they will say their equity. In reality it's their gain. Let's compare the two sets of figures." Table 1-1 shows the comparison Leon made.

"You can see clearly that in your case, gain and equity are, in fact, quite different."

"I still don't see how that can be," Marge said.

"It just isn't possible that we would have to pay taxes on more than we actually made," Peter added.

"More than you actually made?" Leon asked quizzically. "I wonder. Let me ask you something. How do you happen to have such a high loan on your property? Your loan balance is nearly $38,000, yet you say you only paid $20,000 years ago when you bought."

TABLE 1-1 EQUITY VERSUS GAIN

Equity		Gain	
Sales price	$145,000	Sales price	$145,000
Less:		Less allowable costs	9,000
Commission	7,250		
Closing costs	2,000		
	135,750	Adjusted sales price	136,000
Less mortgages	37,750	Less adjusted basis	21,000
Equity	$ 98,000	Gain	$115,000

"That's easily explained," Peter replied. "A few years ago when real estate jumped in value, we decided to take some money out of our house. We refinanced and got well over $20,000 in cash. We bought a car and some furniture and took a 2-week cruise in the Caribbean. It was the best-spent money we ever had."

"Did you think that money was tax-free?" Leon asked.

"Certainly," Marge replied. "We just borrowed it on our house. Why should we pay tax on money we borrowed?"

"You shouldn't," Leon replied. "Not at the time you borrowed it. But you should when it comes time to sell. You see, borrowing money while you own property does not affect the basis, but it does affect the equity. Your borrowing reduced your equity in your home, but your basis remained the same. You might say you've already received that extra gain we were talking about.

"I'm still not clear," Peter said.

"Perhaps an example might help," Leon said. "I can recall a marvelous one that occurred nearly 30 years ago to the first salesperson I ever had. Her name was Inga, and this happened on the first investment property she ever had, a 9-unit apartment building. The price was $90,000, which in those days was big money.

"The owner owed about $60,000. Inga figured the costs of sale including commission at about $9,000.

Sales price of 9 units	$90,000	
Less:		
Current mortgages		$60,000
Costs of sale		9,000
	69,000	$69,000
	$21,000	

"She showed the owner the figures and said that since he would be making a profit of $21,000, he would only have to pay taxes on that amount. Since he had owned the property for nearly 20 years, he could claim a better tax rate through capital gains. It stood to reason he wouldn't have to pay much in the way of taxes. He agreed to sell.

"You can imagine Inga's chagrin when the owner called her up next year at tax time, raving mad. It turned out he had a horrendous tax bill which ate up *all* of the $21,000 profit he had made and more! She showed me the calculations his accountant had made. It turned out that he had bought the property for $30,000 after costs. Over the 20 years of ownership he had lowered the basis through depreciation* by $20,000. That meant that at sale time his adjusted basis was just $10,000!

Purchase price of nine units	$30,000
Less depreciation over 20 years	20,000
Adjusted basis	$10,000!

"He didn't know and Inga had not told him that depreciation lowers the adjusted basis. Since his basis was $10,000, here'e what his tax liability looked like:

Current sales price	$90,000
Less sales expenses	9,000
Adjusted sales price	81,000
Less adjusted basis	10,000
Taxable gain	$71,000

"He had to pay taxes on $71,000, even though at the time of the sale he only netted about $21,000."

"But I still don't understand," Marge said. "Why did he only net out $21,000? If his basis was $10,000, why didn't he net out close to $71,000?"

"Oh, didn't I explain that?" Leon said smiling. "I must be getting old. The reason is that a year before the sale, he refinanced. He got a new mortgage for $50,000 on the property. He had put that money in the bank.

"But, because he had *borrowed* that money, he never thought of it as profit. I explained to him that when he added the $50,000 from the loan money to the $21,000 in cash from the sale, he did in fact come

---

*"Depreciation" simply means the allowance made for anticipated reduction in value. Eventually the nine units would be so old and decrepit that they couldn't be rented. The building would be a total loss. The government allows the owner to capitalize this loss or spread it out over the entire period of ownership.

up with $71,000 (not, of course, including the costs of the refinance). He eventually calmed down."

"That means, then," Peter said, "that because we refinanced our home, our calculations for profit and gain are far apart?"

"Yes, indeed," Leon commented. "Mistaking equity for gain is the biggest mistake that most people make. It is particularly the case on a refinance. I've seen people who have refinanced their homes 5 years earlier and long ago spent the money from that refinance. Now, when they sell, they figure their profit the same as their equity—the difference between the existing loan balance and the sale price.

"They either don't realize or have forgotten that refinancing *during ownership* does not affect their basis. (They can't even add the costs of such refinancing to the basis.) When they sell, the gain is calculated on adjusted basis which in most cases goes back to original purchase price, plus or minus other expenses such as we've earlier indicated."

"That must have been what happened to the Owens," Marge said. "They're a couple who lived down the street from us. They sold their house last year for $140,000. At first Mrs. Owens seemed very happy about the sale. Then she became very depressed. At the time she was telling me, I didn't understand. But, I think I do now. Three years ago they refinanced and used the money to buy an investment home. Their mortgage on their house when they sold was about $70,000, but they had bought the property for only $25,000. I guess they had to pay taxes on the gain between the sales price and basis instead of their equity."

"Of course," Leon pointed out, "you really mean the *adjusted* sales price and the *adjusted* basis of the Owens house. That's what you must have in order to accurately figure out gain. But I suspect your suspicions on why Mrs. Owens went from happy to depressed are probably quite accurate."

"Let's get back to our house," Peter said. "As I recall, you figured that our gain would be $115,000. Does that fall within the $100,000 exclusion? Can we exclude $100,000 of that amount?"

Leon looked at them intently for a moment, then said, "Thus far, we've only seen how to calculate gain on the sale of your home. We haven't at all gotten into the exclusion. You must understand that not everyone qualifies for it. There are age and use requirements. You must have lived in it for the appropriate number of years." (Both requirements are discussed in Chapter 2.)

"Finally," Leon said, "I must point out that this exclusion is for *once in a lifetime.* You may only make it once for a sale (or exchange) on a house after July 26, 1978. The once in a lifetime provision essentially means that if you use the full $100,000, that's fine. But, if you use only $95,000, for example, you don't then have $5,000 left over that you can use again. You in essence lose your chance at that $5,000."

"In our case that doesn't apply," said Peter. "The exclusion simply means a savings on the taxes on our gain of $100,000. For us the remaining $15,000 is taxable."

"Not necessarily," Leon replied. (See Chapter 2.) "I'm merely pointing out that for you the choice is made easier by the fact that you're at the maximum $100,000 of the exclusion. But," he pointed out, "the choice is far more difficult for some other people. What if, for example, your gain was only $50,000 on the sale of your house? If you elected to exclude, then you'd end up saving the taxes on the $50,000, but you'd lose the opportunity for the remaining $50,000."

Leon told them about his friend Harold, who had recently sold his home. Harold lived alone and qualified for the exclusion. However, upon sale, Harold's gain was only $23,000. Should he choose to exclude? If he did he would lose the opportunity to later exclude a much higher amount.

Maximum exclusion	$100,000
Less Harold's gain	23,000
Portion of maximum exclusion lost	$ 77,000

Leon said, "What if Harold later on bought a house and after 5 or 10 years, it shot up in value? At that point his gain might indeed be $100,000 or higher, but because he had taken the exclusion earlier, he couldn't benefit from it. Once he took the exclusion he lost forever the remaining amount, in this case $77,000."

"But that seems so harsh," Marge said. "What if he didn't understand what he was doing? What if he later came to believe he made a mistake? Isn't there any way for him to take it all back?"

"Yes, of course there is," Leon commented. "He could choose to revoke the exclusion, if he acted in time."

"At last," Peter said, "we're getting down to the nuts and bolts of it. How do I file for the exclusion itself?"

"Nothing could be simpler," Leon commented. "You just have

your C.P.A. file an IRS form 2119 in the tax year of the sale." Leon showed them a form which had actually been filled out by the IRS.

Form **2119** Department of the Treasury Internal Revenue Service	**Sale or Exchange of Personal Residence** ▶ See Instructions on back. ▶ Attach to Form 1040.	**1979**

Note: Do not include expenses that are deductible as moving expenses on Form 3903.

Name(s) as shown on Form 1040 *Tom White* Your social security number 333 33 3333

			Yes	No
1(a) Date former residence sold ▶ *September 13, 1979*				
(b) Have you ever postponed any gain on the sale or exchange of a personal residence?				✓
(c) Have you ever claimed a credit for purchase or construction of a new principal residence?. . (If "Yes," see Form 5405.)				✓

(e) Were both the old and new properties used as your principal residence?. . . . . . . — Yes ✓

(f) Were any rooms in either residence rented out or used for business at any time?. . . (If "Yes," see note in line 8 and attach computation.) — No ✓

(d) If you were on active duty in the U.S. Armed Forces or outside of the U.S. after the date of sale of former residence, enter dates. From _____ to _____

(g) If you were married, do you and your spouse have the same proportionate ownership interest in your new residence as you had in your old residence? . . . (If "No," see the Consent below.)

(e) If married at time of sale, was the residence owned by: ☐ you, ☐ your spouse, ☐ both of you.

3 (a) Were you 55 or over on date of sale?. . . ✓
Was your spouse 55 or over on date of sale? . N/A

(f) Social security number of spouse at time of sale, if different from number on Form 1040 ▶

(b) If you answered "Yes" to 3(a), did you own and use the property sold as your principal residence for a total of at least 3 years (except for short temporary absences) of the 5-year period before the sale? . . . . ✓ (If you are 65 or over, see instruction C.)

2(a) Date new residence was bought ▶ N/A

(b) If new residence was constructed by you, date construction began ▶

(c) Date you occupied new residence ▶ N/A

(c) If you answered "Yes" to 3(b), do you elect to exclude gain on the sale from your gross income? . . ✓ (If "Yes," check Yes box and fill in lines 15–20 below.)

(d) If you answered "Yes" to 1(c), did anyone live in your new replacement residence before you did? . . — Yes No

Computation of Gain and Adjusted Sales Price

4 Selling price of residence. (Do not include selling price of personal property items.)	**4**	130,000
5 Commissions and other expenses of sale	**5**	10,000
6 Amount realized (subtract line 5 from line 4)	**6**	120,000
7 Basis of residence sold **7** 50,000		
8 Gain on sale (subtract line 7 from line 6). If line 7 is more than line 6 there is no gain. Do not complete the rest of form. A loss on the sale of a personal residence is not deductible . . . **8** 70,000		
Note: Do not include in line 8 the amount attributable to rented rooms or other business purposes; instead, report separately on Form 4797.		
9 Fixing-up expenses	**9**	NONE
10 Adjusted sales price (subtract line 9 from line 6)	**10**	120,000

Computation of Gain to be Reported and Adjusted Basis of New Residence
(Complete lines 11 through 14 if you did not check "Yes" to question 3(c).)

11 Cost of new residence	**11**	
12 Gain taxable this year (line 10 less line 11, but not more than line 8). If line 11 is more than line 10, enter zero. Enter on Schedule D (Form 1040), line 1 or 9, column g	**12**	
13 Gain on which tax is to be postponed (subtract line 12 from line 8)	**13**	
14 Adjusted basis of new residence (subtract line 13 from line 11)	**14**	

Exclusion, Gain to be Reported, and Adjusted Basis of New Residence
(For use of taxpayers 55 years of age or over who checked "Yes" in 3(c) above.)

15 Exclusion: Enter the smaller of line 8 or $100,000 ($50,000, if married filing separately)	**15**	70,000
16 Part of gain included (subtract line 15 from line 8)	**16**	NONE
17 Cost of new residence. If a new personal residence was not bought, enter "None," and do not complete the rest of form. Enter the amount from line 16 on Schedule D (Form 1040), line 9, column g.	**17**	NONE
18 Gain taxable this year. (Subtract the sum of lines 15 and 17 from line 10.) This amount may not be more than line 16. If line 17 plus line 15 is more than line 10, enter zero. Enter here and on Schedule D (Form 1040), line 9, column g	**18**	
19 Gain on which tax is to be postponed (subtract line 18 from line 16)	**19**	
20 Adjusted basis of new residence (subtract line 19 from line 17)	**20**	

Consent of You and Your Spouse to Apply Separate Gain on Sale of Old Residence to Basis of New Residence
(Applies only if you and your same spouse use both residences as your principal residence. See instruction D.)

The undersigned taxpayers, you and your spouse, consent to have the basis of the joint or separate interest in the new residence reduced by the amount of the joint or separate gain on the sale of the old residence which is not taxable only because of the filing of this Consent.

Your signature ▶ _____ Date ▶ _____

Spouse's signature ▶ _____ Date ▶ _____

		Your part	Spouse's part
21 Adjusted sales price of old residence (from line 10)	**21**		
22 Cost of new residence (from line 11 or 17)	**22**		

Form 2119 used to report sale or exchange of residence

"Of course," Leon pointed out, "we mustn't put the cart before the horse. You can't get the exclusion unless you and the property qualify.

"There are a lot of people who really want to know if they do, in fact, qualify for the up to $100,000 exclusion. I have a broker friend who's holding an informal meeting to answer people's questions on the qualification for the exclusion. I suggest you attend."

T W O

Finding Out Whether You Qualify for the Up to $100,000 Exclusion

Marge and Peter decided to go to the meeting Leon had told them about. It was in a neighbor's house about five blocks away. The speaker was Leonard, a real estate broker with a legal background.

After refreshments were passed out, Leonard said that probably the best way to learn who did or did not qualify for the $100,000 exclusion was for the members of the audience to ask him questions. They could describe their particular situation and then he could give them a specific answer. (In a similar fashion, you, the reader, may find out whether you qualify by reading the questions and answers.)

Leonard pointed out, however, that while his answers were based on his best information available at the time, the interpretation of the law changes frequently as new court cases are decided. He cautioned that his audience (including you, the reader) should not rely on his answers, but should also consult directly with their own attorney before making any legal or tax decision.

Everyone was hesitant to begin, but finally Marge raised her hand and asked:

BASIC RULE

Question: What is the basic rule for qualifying for the exclusion?

Answer: There are both age and use qualifications. Basically, the person filing for the exclusion must be 55 years of age on the day the sale closes (title

---

This chapter was prepared with the assistance of Norman H. Lane, professor of tax law at the University of Southern California Law Center.

changes) and must have lived in the principal residence for three out of the past five years.

AGE

Question: I didn't know about the rule when I sold my house last year, and I was 55 years old one day after the sale was closed. Does that rule me out?

Answer: No, the law actually interprets you to be 55 one day before your fifty-fifth birthday, so you would still qualify.

THREE OUT OF FIVE YEARS

Question: Let's get back to that three out of five years rule you were talking about. I have a house that I'm selling and I plan to take the exclusion. Only for the past three years, I've gone on a vacation for a couple of months during the summer and rented the house out each time. Since I've only owned the house for a total of three years, I need all my time in it to qualify. Am I prevented from claiming the exclusion because I took vacations and rented the property out?

Answer: You may still claim the exclusion. The rule generally is that if you take a vacation for up to a couple of months, even if you rent the property out during that time, it is considered occupying the residence.

LONG ABSENCES

Question: What about me? I'm a teacher and last year I took a sabbatical. I left the country and rented my house out for a year. Does that year I was gone still qualify me under the use requirements?

Answer: No. Generally speaking the IRS says that if you're gone for such an extended period of time, you could not claim the house during that year. Of course, you could always fight it out in tax court, but generally the rule is if you stay away more than a couple of months, you "break the chain."

PRINCIPAL RESIDENCE

Question: A few minutes ago you said something I didn't understand. You described the house as the "principal residence." What did you mean by that?

Answer: The law says that you may take this exclusion only on your principal residence or what the Internal Revenue Service sometimes calls your "main home." What they mean by your principal residence is the home that you have maintained as your main residence. You can have only one, and you must have maintained it as your main residence for three out of the last five years.

Question: The reason I asked the last question is because I don't own a house. I own a condominium. Does the law apply to condos as well as to houses?

Answer: Yes, it does. Many types of homes satisfy the principal residence requirement, including houses, condominiums, unit ownerships in a stock cooperative, and mobile homes. Yachts and houseboats have been ruled main houses in some instances. It is possible, although far from certain, that you might even be able to claim a large van or motor home as your principal residence—although in a case such as that, you might have to fight the IRS.

PART-INVESTMENT PROPERTY

Question: What about my case? I own a duplex. I live in one unit and rent the other unit out. Can I claim the entire property as my principal residence?

Answer: No, not the entire property. The law does, however, allow you to claim that portion in which you do actually reside. If it is an identical duplex, then making the calculation should be very simple for you. Since you reside in one-half of the building, if you otherwise meet the age and use requirements, you can exclude up to one-half of the gain.

Question: I'm still not clear on that. Are you saying that because I only own one-half of the building, I can only claim $50,000 instead of $100,000?

Answer: Not at all. I'm saying that you can claim one-half of the *gain* up to $100,000. Let's suppose that you sell your duplex, and your gain (see Chapter 1 for an explanation of gain) is $180,000. You must now cut that gain in half (since you only live in half the building). That means that you may now exclude $90,000. The other $90,000 would be taxed normally.

Duplex—one-half principal residence use

Gain $180,000 (divided by 2)	$90,000	Portion which may be excluded
	$90,000	Portion which may *not* be excluded

On the other hand, let's say that instead of having a gain on your sale of $180,000, your gain was actually $220,000. When we go to divide the property, we find that we're immediately over the $100,000 mark. However, since $100,000 is the maximum exclusion, that's all you can exclude. The remaining $120,000 must be handled normally.

Many taxpayers normally take depreciation on investment property. The rented portion of the duplex is such investment property, which may already have been depreciated. This lowers the basis on the rented half of the building. The total gain, then, is higher (due to depreciation—see Chapter 1). In this case more than half of the total gain doesn't qualify.

Question: In our case, we live over our store. Can our living area be claimed, even though we're in a commercial building?

Answer: Yes, usually the division is made in terms of area. Let me ask you, what percentage of the total space of the building is used for living area, that is, for your principal residence?

Question: About 30 percent.

Answer: Then you'll be able to claim 30 percent of your gain up to $100,000 on the exclusion when it comes time to sell.

TRADES

Question: As long as we're talking about the home, I recently traded my home instead of selling it. Because I didn't receive any cash and because it was a trade, does that mean I can't claim the exclusion?

Answer: You may still claim it. A trade, for purposes of the exclusion, is treated as if it were a sale of your old house and purchase of a new one. If you otherwise qualify, you may claim the exclusion on your gain.

ONLY ONE SPOUSE QUALIFIES

Question: I want to get back to the matter of who qualifies for the exclusion. My husband and I sold our home last month. I am 56 years old, but he is only 53. We've both lived in the house for three out of the past five years, and so we qualify. But, are we eliminated from the exclusion because only one of us is 55 while the other is younger?

Answer: You still qualify. If only one spouse satisfies the age rule, then both of you do, even if one is younger than 55. But, you both must claim it jointly.

Question: You said that only one spouse had to be 55 years old. Well, I'm 57, but my husband is only 51. Can I claim the exclusion, because I qualify, and leave my husband out? By that I mean, can he not claim it so that he could use it at some later date?

Answer: No. Both husband and wife must claim the exemption regardless of the fact that one may be younger.

PRIOR EXCLUSION, DEATH OF SPOUSE

Question: Along those lines, let's say I am an unmarried man. By that I mean I was married years earlier and then my wife died. We had already sold a home on which we satisfied the age and use requirements and we had claimed the exclusion.

Now, let's say that years later I find a lovely woman and marry her. We settle down in another house. Maybe 10 years from now we decide to sell. I took the exclusion when I was unmarried on another house. She never took the exclusion at all. Do we qualify?

Answer: Questions regarding marital status can be the most complicated. I hope that more of you will ask them so I'll have an opportunity to respond.

To specifically answer your question, no, you may not take the exclusion. If both you and your new wife own the property as joint tenants or tenants by entirety, or if it is community property, then you *must* both join in the choice to exclude. Since you've already excluded before, you are barred from excluding again.

PRIOR CLAIM BY ONE SPOUSE

Question: But, to repeat my question, what about the fact that my present wife never joined in my original exclusion? Doesn't she have the right to exclude up to $100,000?

Answer: No. By marrying, this woman becomes your spouse, and the rule is that this exclusion on the sale or exchange of property may *not* be claimed if either taxpayer or spouse has already taken it.

BOTH HUSBAND AND WIFE MUST JOIN

Question: I think you've opened up a can of worms with your last answer. Consider my situation. I'm the wife of the man who was just asking the questions. I have a house that is my own separate property (not community property, not jointly owned). Can I declare that separate house my principal residence and, if I satisfy the use requirements, get up to a $100,000 exclusion on gain for it?

Answer: Once again, no, for the same reason I've just given. Any election by a taxpayer who's married requires that it be joined in by the spouse. If you were a single or unmarried woman, it would be different. But, since you're married, your husband must join you in getting the exclusion.

REVOKING EXCLUSION

Question: I'm the husband of the woman who just asked that question, and I'm still in trouble. Since we can't get the exclusion on our present house and since she can't even get it on her separate property, is there any way that I can revoke the exclusion I took before when I was previously married?

Answer: Yes, the exclusion may be revoked. The time period for revocation is normally the same period of time you have for claiming a refund on your taxes. It is normally 3 years from the date of filing of the return for the year of sale or April 15th, whichever is later.

TIME FOR REVOCATION

Question: You mean, I have three years to revoke the exclusion?

Answer: That could be deceptive. You may actually have longer depending on when you sold your house. The time limit starts not from the date of the sale but, as I just indicated, from the date you filed your tax return on April 15th of the tax year the house was sold in, whichever is later. (The effect of revoking, however, is that you'll now have to pay capital gains tax on your gain.)

DIVORCE

Question: The questions this couple were asking are similar to one I have. I'm getting a divorce. Both my former husband and I are over 55, and we satisfy the use requirements. Because we are divorcing, however, can we *each* claim $100,000?

Answer: It depends on the status of your divorce proceedings. If you have a *final* divorce decree in effect prior to the sale (not just an interlocutory decree), then, presumably each of you would be unmarried individuals. Each of you could claim up to $100,000. Let's say that your house is sold after your divorce decree and that you each get $80,000 of gain from the sale. You would each be eligible to claim the exclusion on the entire $80,000.

When divorce is final

Total gain on house	$160,000	
Gain for spouse 1	$80,000	Full amount may
Gain for spouse 2	$80,000	be excluded.

On the other hand, let's say that you were merely separated or had an interlocutory decree. In other words, your divorce was *not yet final* at the time of sale. In that case, you would have to limit your combined exclusion to $100,000 if you were filing a joint return, or $50,000 apiece on separate returns.

When divorce is not final

Total gain on house	$160,000	(Assuming separate returns)	
Gain for spouse 1	$80,000	amount excluded	$50,000
Gain for spouse 2	$80,000	amount excluded	$50,000

Question: I have something to ask similar to this. I'm now married to a wonderful woman. I was formerly married and two years ago was divorced. I took the exclusion with my former wife when we sold our house upon our divorce.

But now, I have a new wife and another house which I'm thinking of selling. I want to take the exclusion with my new wife on my new house. I believe you said that since I had already chosen it before, I can't take it again, even though my new wife never has?

Answer: That's correct.

JOINT REVOCATION IN DIVORCE

Question: But you also said there was a provision for revoking my former exclusion. Since I still fall within the time limits for revoking you mentioned earlier, can't I now revoke the exclusion on my former house?

Answer: Yes, you can. However, you may have a problem. The law specifically states that an exclusion can only be revoked by those who made it. If you made a joint exclusion, then in order to revoke it, both you and your former wife would have to agree to do so. You couldn't do it entirely on your own.

Question: You don't know my former wife. Isn't there some way I could revoke without having to ask her?

Answer: She must join you in the revocation. Perhaps if you offered to work out a settlement along money lines, it might be accomplished.

REPAYMENT OF TAXES IN REVOCATION

Question: I doubt it. But what you said brings up another question. What if she were to join me in the revocation? Would we then have to pay the taxes we originally saved by claiming the exclusion?

Answer: Yes, you'd be responsible for all the taxes you didn't have to pay because you claimed the exclusion.

Question: Then revoking could be expensive.

Answer: It could be. You certainly wouldn't want to do it unless you had a very good reason.

DEATH OF SPOUSE PRIOR TO SALE—NO REMARRIAGE

Question: I have a question different from this gentleman who was just talking. My husband died recently. We were both over 55 and fulfilled the use requirements. Can I claim the exclusion on the house?

Answer: This is a very difficult question to answer, though it sounds simple. I strongly recommend professional advice in any case where death of a spouse has occurred within three years of the date of sale.

To understand my answer, you have to realize that, in general, where a couple has "co-owned" property at the time of the death of one, whether as joint tenants, tenants by entirety, community property, or tenants in common, the tax law regards the single house as two separate properties which I will call *H*'s half and *W*'s half. The ownership and use qualifications for each half must be determined separately for three years after the death of one, even though the survivor acquires full title to the entire property.

If you live in a community property state and held the house as community property when *H* dies, then both halves of the house get a "stepped-up" basis equal to fair market value at the time of death or, in some cases, shortly thereafter. Since the basis is stepped-up the taxable gain is reduced without regard to the special $100,000 exclusion and if the house is not sold for much more than that "date of death value," it would be unwise to make the election. In some cases, however, substantial appreciation may occur between the date of death and the date of sale and you may wish to make the election.

The basic principle is that W's half qualifies for the election if at the time of sale she is over 55 years old, has owned her half for three of the past five years and has used the house as her principal residence during that period. H's half qualifies for the election only if at the date of sale W is over 55 and H had (1) owned his half of the property and (2) occupied it as his principal residence for three of the five years before the date of sale (not the date of his death). If the parties had owned the house and lived in it for three years prior to death and the sale is made within two years of H's death, then the requirements will normally be met on both halves and both halves qualify for the election. The main problem would be if H had made an election (after July 26, 1978) on his other residence which was in force at his death; in such case, H's half would not qualify for the election. Also if W is remarried at the time of sale, his half doesn't qualify. If the sale is more than two years after H dies, then H's half would not qualify for the election. H obviously cannot meet the 3-out-of-5-year test, since he won't have been alive for three of the past five years. In such a case, only W's half might qualify for the exclusion. Whether one half or both halves qualify, the maximum amount of the exclusion is $100,000; also, if both halves qualify then W's election will apply to both halves.

Note that if W waits more than three years after H's death to sell the house, then she individually will usually have (1) owned the entire house and (2) occupied it as her residence, for three of the five years prior to sale. Accordingly, her entire gain qualifies for the exclusion and H's status is irrelevant. Problems can arise, of course, if W moves out of the house before selling it. The danger area is thus the sale between 2 and 3 years after H's death.

Again assuming a community property state, if the parties held the property "as joint tenants" rather than as community property, then only H's half and not W's half gets a stepped up basis at H's death. Thus the $100,000 exclusion may well be more important since there is a greater taxable gain to be concerned about. However, all the other rules mentioned still apply. Qualification for both halves must be determined separately until W's period of sole ownership is at least three years and H's half can't qualify once two years pass from the date of his death. The two- to three-year interval is very dangerous.

In a separate property state, we often find that both halves get a stepped-up basis, even though the property was held as joint tenants; often, however, this is at the cost of paying additional estate tax. Where the parties hold as joint tenants or tenants by the entirety, qualification for each half must still be determined separately under the foregoing principles, until W's period of sole ownership is at least three years.

In some cases the deceased spouse may have owned the residence as his separate property, which passes to the surviving spouse by will or intestate succession. This can even occur in a community property state, particularly in the case of people who marry late in life. Where the deceased spouse was the sole owner for income tax purposes, then, until the survivor can individually qualify for a three-year holding and use period, qualification for any exclusion requires that (1) the survivor is at least 55 years old at the time of sale and has not remarried, (2) the decedent satisfied the holding and use requirements for three of the five years preceding the sale, and (3) the decedent had not made a previous, post-1978 election. This means usually, but not always, that the entire gain will qualify for the exclusion if the sale is made within two or more than three years after the decedent dies, but will not qualify if it occurs in the interim period. Furthermore, where the decedent was the sole owner of the house at the time of his death, the entire property qualifies for a stepped-up basis, so the exclusion is generally less important.

While the preceding discussion may seem unnecessarily complex, please note that it is because the law is very complex at this point. This is why I must emphasize again that professional advice is indispensable if you are actually confronted with one of these situations.

SINGLE PERSON

Question: I'm a single woman and I've lived in my home the last three out of five years. Because I'm not married, do I only get half the exclusion, or $50,000?

Answer: Single men or women get up to the full $100,000 exclusion just the same as married couples.

Question: Are you sure about that? It doesn't seem fair that one person should get the same exclusion as two.

Answer: The law is quite specific. Whether you're married or single, the exclusion is up to $100,000. Although, if you're married, both husband and wife must elect to take it jointly.

THREE OUT OF FIVE YEARS NOT CONTINUOUS

Question: My question is totally different from those asked by these other people who have spoken. I simply want to know if the three out of five years has to be continuous?

Answer: Certainly not. All you have to show is that you lived in the property for 36 full months or 1,095 days (365 × 3).

At this point the hostess indicated that it was time for a coffee break. Marge talked over what had been said with Peter. He indicated that it certainly did seem as if they would qualify. They both were over 55 and they both had lived in the house for 20 years. There wasn't any problem there. He did, however, have one question which hadn't come up. When they sold, he figured he could "roll over" the house. He had heard that if you sell one house and buy another within a certain period of time for more money, all the tax you would have to pay on the gain of the old house is deferred somehow to the new one. Since they'd be getting a gain of over $100,000, he thought this might be a way of not having to immediately pay any taxes at all. Marge urged Peter to ask the question, but he was a bit shy and decided to wait until later.

The first person to raise her hand after the break asked a question relating back to what they had discussed earlier.

TENANTS IN COMMON

Question: You said that if a husband and wife wanted the exclusion, they had to join in the choice. My situation is somewhat different. I and my brother and sister live together in our house. On sale the gain will probably be over $270,000. My sister and I qualify for the age and use requirements. But my brother, who is over 55, has only lived with us for about a year and cannot meet the use requirements. We own the house as tenants in common and we'll split the gain when it's sold.

My question is, do we all together get a $100,000 exclusion, or does each of us get it separately? And what about my brother?

Answer: Since the house is not community property (because there is no marriage involved) and since it is not owned in entirety or as joint tenants, you do not have to join with one another in order to get the exclusion. That means that since you and your sister each meet the age and use qualifications, you can each take up to $100,000. However, since your brother does not meet the use qualifications, he cannot claim any exclusion at all.

Gain on house—$270,000 divided three ways:

Sister 1	$90,000	(May be excluded)
Sister 2	$90,000	(May be excluded)
Brother	$90,000	(May *not* be excluded)

EXECUTOR

Question: Going back to what you were saying earlier about someone who died, I have an uncle who died recently and I'm the executor of his estate. He had a house in which he lived for 20 years, and he was 73 when he died so he obviously met the age and use qualifications.

Just before he died he put his house up for sale, but he had a fatal heart attack before the deal was completed. It was sold, that is, title was transferred after his death. Now I'm trying to settle his estate and I have a big tax burden to handle on the property. As his executor, can I claim the exclusion for him?

Answer: No, you probably can't. The law is not quite clear here, but in general, an executor cannot make the exclusion claim on the behalf of the deceased if it is the executor who sells the house. The executor cannot do it even if the deceased fully qualified, even if he entered into a contract for the sale prior to his death. In analogous situations, some courts have overruled the IRS.

You should note, however, that if the decedent had not entered into a binding contract to sell the property before his death, but had merely listed the property with a broker, or if the contract were subject to numerous unfulfilled conditions when death occurred, then the basis of the property would be "stepped-up" to its fair market value on the date of death and there would be no gain to report.

DOUBLE EXCLUSION FROM PRIOR SALE

Question: What if the sale was complete prior to his death? Can I now claim it as his executor?

Answer: In this case, since the sale was completed before death, the exclusion may be claimed on the decedent's final return. Either you or another person may have been appointed executor or administrator by a probate court. In this case the final return including the election has to be made by the duly authorized representative, either individually or by joining in a final joint return. If no probate was required, you as the surviving spouse may file the final return (including a joint return) on behalf of your husband and claim the election there.

Question: I have what I believe is an unusual question. Am I correct in assuming that prior to the passage of the law we're now talking about, the government allowed a different kind of exclusion for the elderly?

Answer: That is correct. Prior to July 27, 1978 a person who was 65 years or older and who had lived in a main house for five out of eight years could qualify for an exclusion of up to $35,000.

Question: Well, I'm nearly seventy now and when I was 65 I did take that exclusion. Because I took the earlier exclusion, am I now barred from claiming this new once-in-a-lifetime $100,000 exclusion on the sale of my present house?

Answer: In your case, you may claim *both* the earlier exclusion and the present one. However, a person can only claim each exclusion once.

Question: I'm rather shocked by what I just heard this man ask and you answer. And also I'm wondering if I can really save some money here. I sold my home before the new law took effect. I've since bought a second home which I'm not selling. Do you mean to tell me that I can go back and still claim the up to $35,000 exclusion on my first home as well as get the up to $100,000 exclusion on my current home?

Answer: If you sold your first home before July 27, 1978, and otherwise qualify, you can get the up to $35,000 exclusion. I must point out, however, that the last possible date for filing for this is three years from April 15th of the year the sale took place. That would be April 15, 1982.

If you sold your second home after July 26, 1978, then you would also qualify for the up to $100,000 exclusion we've been discussing.

I should point out, however, that the qualifications for the earlier up to $35,000 exclusion were substantially different from the current rule. They required that you live in the home for five out of eight years. The calculation for the exclusion was also made very differently. I suggest you see your accountant or tax attorney to get special help if you're concerned about this area.

TRANSITION RULE

Question: Along the lines the last gentleman was asking, I had heard that there was a "transition rule'' that I might use since I do not qualify for the three out of five years. Could you tell me what it is?

Answer: The transition rule is that people who do not meet the three-out-of-five-years requirement for the current $100,000 exclusion may, under certain circumstances, qualify by using the old five-out-of-eight-years formula. However, again this is a technical area and you should see your personal accountant or attorney. Also, this transition rule expired July 26, 1981.

CONDEMNATION

Question: My house was condemned to make way for a new highway. Does that constitute a sale on which I can take the exclusion?

Answer: Yes, if you otherwise qualify.

Question: As it turns out, I only lived in the house 2 years, so I don't qualify. But I've since bought another house in which I've lived for one year. Can I add the two years in the house that was condemned to the one year in my present house for the required three-year use period?

Answer: Yes, you can, but only because the house was an *involuntary sale* (you didn't choose to sell of your own free will).

First house	2 years	(involuntary conversion)
Second house	1 year	
	3 years	Qualifies

At this point, Peter stood and asked his roll-over question:

EXCLUSION COMBINED WITH ROLL-OVER

Question: I understand that the government has a rule whereby if I sell my house and then, within a certain time period, buy another house for more money, I don't have to pay tax on any of the gain on the house I sell, but instead can transfer it to the new house. When I sell I am going to have more than $100,000 gain. While I qualify and so will be able to exclude the first $100,000, presumably I'll have to pay taxes on the remainder. But I plan to buy another house. Here's my question: Is there some way I can combine this $100,000 exclusion with the roll-over I've just described so I don't have to pay any taxes at all?

Answer: I'm glad you brought that up. This very well may be one of the most advantageous aspects of the new exclusion rule for those over 55.

First, let's describe more clearly what you call a "roll-over." Technically it's called a "nonrecognition of gain." What it means is that the gain you get from selling your old house is *deferred* to your new house. Actually, you don't get out of paying taxes; you just postpone them.

I must mention that this nonrecognition-of-gain rule, while not complicated, has many facets, and to fully describe it would take a long time. Therefore, please keep in mind that what I am saying is not even the bare minimum and you must see an accountant or tax attorney before using the rule.

The nonrecognition rule states in part that if you sell your principal residence and then replace it with another within 18 months prior to or after the sale of your old house (up to 24 months after the sale for new construction), *and* the new house costs more in price than the old, then you may defer (postpone) all the gain on the sale of the old house. (If the new house costs less than the old, some of the gain may still be postponed.)

I am sure that most of you are somewhat familiar with this rule. It's the one that allows you to not pay taxes when you sell your house as long as you buy a more expensive house.

The elderly have always had a problem with this rule. Let's take an example. You, who asked the question, would you mind giving us your tax situation?

Peter stood up and explained their gain. He said that they were selling their house for an adjusted sales price of $136,000. Their gain was $115,000

(Chapter 1 explains how they arrived at their gain). Leonard thanked Peter for his explanation and then went on. Under the old nonrecognition rule, in order to defer the entire gain, you would have to now buy a house costing *more* than $115,000. However, at retirement age most people want to cash in their house and get into something less expensive. The rule, therefore, would work against you.

However, the new $100,000 exclusion can be combined with the nonrecognition rule. Here's how it works:

Adjusted sales price of old home

Old home price	$136,000
Less $100,000 exclusion	100,000
	$36,000

Now you need only buy a home for $36,000 or more to defer the remainder of the gain, which in your case was $15,000.

Total gain	$115,000
Less exclusion	100,000
	$ 15,000

It is this combining of the up to $100,000 exclusion with the nonrecognition of gain that allows older people to "step down" into smaller homes in many cases without having to pay any taxes at all.

Peter was certainly glad he had asked the question. It was growing late and it appeared to be almost time to go. Leonard said, "We have time for one more question.

EXCLUSION COMBINED WITH INSTALLMENT SALE

Question: I'm going to sell my house under the installment plan. Can the exclusion be used in conjunction with it in the same way it was for the nonrecognition rule you just described?

Answer: Yes, it can. First, let me explain the installment plan. It also has many facets, and my explanation will necessarily be brief and will not cover it all. So again check with your accountant or tax attorney. Basically, under the installment plan when you sell and receive your total money (including some mortgages and cash) in more than one year, then you may spread out the payment of taxes according to the payments made by the buyer. Would you please tell us your name and the type of sale you plan?

Question: I'm John and I have a house with an adjusted sales price of $200,000. My adjusted basis is $40,000, so I have $160,000 gain. I plan to get $50,000 in cash and spread the remainder of the proceeds of the house out over five years.

Adjusted sales price	$200,000
Adjusted basis	40,000
Gain	$160,000
Down payment	$ 50,000

As I understand the rule, I have to pay taxes for the year of the sale only on the $50,000. I can pay taxes on the remaining gain in the following 5 years as I get it, according to a complicated formula my accountant worked out. The reason I'm doing this is because if I took all the gain at once, it would bump me up into a higher tax bracket. By taking just a bit at a time, I can get into lower brackets and save some money. Now, how does all this work in with the exclusion?

Answer: Quite simply. If you qualify, you just take the $100,000 off the top.

Gain	$160,000
Less exclusion	100,000
Remaining gain	$ 60,000

Your accountant will show you how to spread that $60,000 remaining gain over the five years period. With capital gains, you should have a relatively small tax liability. I think the important point raised by your question is that the $100,000 exclusion can be used in conjunction with the installment sale plan.

Then the meeting broke up, and Marge and Peter began talking while they walked home. From what they had learned, they could sell their present home and get all the money out without paying any taxes, provided they bought another home at a fairly low cost. The decision now was, should they sell?

THREE

Finding the Best Retirement Housing

Marge and Peter spent a long time thinking about what Leon and the attorney had said. They now knew that they could claim the up to $100,000 exclusion on their gain, but they would have to sell their present home to get it. If they bought another home, they probably could even defer the taxes on the remainder of the gain. Now, however, tax savings somehow didn't seem to be what bothered them. Their concern was that in order to get the benefits of the exclusion, they'd have to sell their home. "Can we stand to sell our very own home?" Marge lamented.

Peter pointed out that selling a place in which they'd lived for so many years was, indeed, a big decision. They had picked out their house so it would be big enough for their children to grow up in. Every room was filled with memories. Even the chips in the paint and the cracks in the tile told stories of where their children had played. "How can we even begin to think of giving up this house?" Marge repeated.

Peter pointed out that there were some problems with keeping it. The most important was the fact that it was so large. Their home had four bedrooms, but now that their children were gone they really only needed one and perhaps a guest room. "We can't sleep in more than one bedroom at a time," Peter pointed out.

He also indicated that they were paying higher taxes because their large house was worth so much. If they had a smaller house, then presumably, their taxes would be lower. An important consideration.

Finally, he said that the housework was keeping them both busy far too much. They wanted to spend their time now in taking trips and enjoying themselves. They didn't want to have to spend so much of it in cleaning.

"Talk about cleaning," Peter said. "It takes me one full day a week just to mow the lawns and trim the bushes outside. If anyone thinks that's a pleasure, they're crazy."

"But," Marge pointed out, "you've also got the garden you planted. You enjoy working in it, don't you?"

Peter nodded that he did.

Finally, they decided to contact Karen, the woman who had led the retirement seminar at Peter's company. She had indicated she would be happy to talk more with anyone who wanted additional counseling.

When they met Karen at her office, she told them she specialized in helping people make retirement decisions and she had retired herself just a few years earlier. "My role is to present alternatives," Karen said.

"It's understandable that you would feel a sense of loss at the prospect of leaving your present home." Karen said. "It's like a treasured, well-fitting garment. It feels comfortable. You know it well. Selling and moving to new surroundings can be traumatic. As a matter of fact, if the move is not made carefully, studies show that you can actually have an extended period of depression caused just by leaving your old home. Psychologists say that three of the most difficult changes that most people have to handle in life are divorce, a change of job, and a change of home, not necessarily in that order."

"But," Marge pointed out, "there are many reasons why we do want to leave. The house is too big for us now, and we are overburdened with the maintenance, to name just two."

Karen nodded, then said, "I think it's helpful to come to a clear understanding of what retirement really is."

TWO STAGES OF RETIREMENT

"Perhaps the most helpful way to think of retirement is in two stages, although most people fail to see this. The first stage is what I call 'active retirement.' It is the years immediately after you stop working when you can actively pursue interests such as hobbies and travel and physical recreation. You may want to spend part of each day swimming or golfing or doing some other activity you always liked but never had time for before. And perhaps you'll want to spend months out of each year traveling either in this country or abroad. During the active period, health is a relatively minor concern.

"All of us, however, eventually experience a second stage of retirement, which might be called 'elderly retirement.' Please keep in mind I'm not talking specific ages here. This second stage may not occur until we're 80 or 90, or for some it may occur in the sixties or earlier. What it amounts to is a time when our mobility is reduced, when we find we want to spend long periods of time resting or sleeping, and when medical problems can become a serious concern.

"A person who is considering retirement must realize that chances are he or she will have to eventually go through the second stage as well as the first. What I'm getting at," Karen concluded, "is that in choosing a retirement house, a wise person will consider both stages. The choice may be made in such a way that the home can satisfy both the first and the second stages of retirement. Or the purchase can be made with the understanding that the home is very temporary with another choice planned for later on. Going with the first way, however, saves having to go hunting for a new home again just when you're least able to do so, when you're entering the second stage."

"What you're saying," Peter spoke up, "is that it only makes sense to plan ahead."

"That's exactly right," Karen said. "When you look for a retirement home you should not just consider your immediate needs. You should also consider your needs a few years down the road."

"It sounds to me," Peter said, "as if what you're pushing is a retirement community. A place where a bunch of old people sit around in the sun all day."

Karen smiled, "That's not at all what I meant. You may indeed like a retirement community. Then, again, you may not. It certainly isn't for everyone. Or you may find that simply staying where you are is the best alternative for you. I'm merely saying that you should consider where you'll be in terms of your true needs. For example, let's take your present house."

REASONS FOR LEAVING PRESENT HOME

"You've already told me two things that you currently find wrong with the house: It's too big and there's too much maintenance."

"That's right," Marge said, "even though it's filled with memories, all those empty rooms give me a lonely feeling. I simply leave the doors to most of the bedrooms closed. Besides, if we're not using the place, why should we be cleaning it and paying taxes on it?''

"And, of course, the yardwork and other maintenance is a full-time job," Peter said, "although I have the time to do it now, so I guess I shouldn't complain."

"But," Karen asked, "will you always feel like doing it or be able to do it? At some time in the future will you have to hire someone to do most of the maintenance for you? What about the costs involved in that?''

Karen then asked about their neighborhood. She pointed out that older neighborhoods sometimes deteriorate. Many older families have found that no matter how well they kept up their homes, the old family house eventually became like an island in a sea of blighted homes. "That's not to say, of course," Karen indicated, "that just because a neighborhood is old, it will go sour. But it has happened so often that it is something to consider."

"Finally," Karen said, "let me ask you this. Are there any physical problems with your present home?"

Marge and Peter looked at each other.

"What I mean," Karen continued, "is something like this. Is your present home two stories tall? Does it have stairs you have to climb?''

Marge noted that it was and that there were even stairs leading to the basement. "It's good you pointed that out," Marge said, "I don't like to have to be always climbing stairs. Sometimes my back goes out and it's difficult."

"Think how difficult it could be in the second stage of retirement," Karen pointed out. "Of course, I'm not trying to talk you out of where you're living. There may also be good reasons for staying where you are."

REASONS FOR STAYING IN PRESENT HOME

The Family and Friends Security Base

"When you move, you are threatened with many things, among them losing some of your friends. Depending on how far you move, you may even lose some of your family in the sense that you won't be able to see them so often."

"I can't believe that," Peter said. "We make new friends so quickly. I'm sure we'd fit in wherever we moved to."

"I'm sure you would too," Karen said, "in time, but the initial adjustment period could take quite a while. Not just a few weeks, but months or even years. You could get very lonesome, particularly if where you moved to turned out not to be what you anticipated.

"Let me give you an example. Where you are now, you know some of your neighbors. You also probably have friends living nearby you can call if you need some little or even some big help. Perhaps your friends drop in on you occasionally to chat. All these social connections form a kind of security system for you. They give you psychological support. If you move any great distance, you will probably rupture them. You will be removing their psychological support, and until you have time to build new friendships, you may not have any support.

"It could be very difficult for a while, particularly if a crisis, such as illness, happened to occur at the same time."

"So what you're saying," Marge said, "is that we shouldn't move far away from our present home?"

"No, I'm not suggesting that," Karen said. "I'm only saying that making a distant move could be perilous. That's why, I suspect, statistics I've seen indicate that as many as 60 to 70 percent of people who retire choose to remain in their former home. They choose not to move at all."

"But," Peter pointed out, "that means that they couldn't get the up to $100,000 exclusion."

"Well," Karen commented, "of course these statistics were taken before the exclusion became law. Perhaps now that it's on the books, we'll see more people selling their homes to take advantage of it."

"In any event, statistics also show that, of those that do move, nearly 90 percent move to a location near their former home. You see, breaking away has proven to be very difficult for many, many people.

"There are also practical problems."

LOGISTICAL PROBLEMS WITH MOVING

"What do you mean by practical problems?" Marge asked.

"Consider," Karen pointed out, "where you are now. You are intimately familiar with where your shopping is located. If you have a car, you know the routes to drive there. If you don't have a car, then I would presume you know the bus or train routes. In either event, you know how to get from your house to every spot you need to go. If you move, however, you'll have to learn all of this sort of thing over again."

"That's not so hard," Peter said.

"It may depend on how old you are. At your relatively young age, it's probably very simple. But, as you get older it can be very difficult. I still have a car, but I'd be afraid to just hop on the freeway and head off to a place I've never been. My eyes aren't as good as they used to be, nor is my hearing. And I'm not as confident about my driving ability. It's a consideration for me."

"Perhaps someday it will be for us, too," Marge said thoughtfully, "but not quite yet."

"There are other problems which I call logistical," Karen continued. "Where you are now you have professional people whom you've known for years and can count on—your real estate broker, your attorney, your accountant, your banker, and perhaps most importantly, your doctor."

"But," Marge pointed out, "there are brokers, attorneys, doctors, and such everywhere we go. It's not like we're planning on moving to the North Pole. These services are readily available."

"Perhaps they are," Karen continued, "but consider this. When you move to a new area you are particularly vulnerable. You may not know the best areas or what to pay for a house. You may need legal advice as well as investment advice, yet you may not know an attorney or a banker. Finally, what if you have some chronic illness? Moving away from your current physician can be traumatic. How do you know you'll find another doctor who will want to continue the same method of treatment or will be sympathetic to your needs?"

Marge and Peter looked at each other. Finally Marge said, "From what you're saying, it appears we really shouldn't move at all."

Karen smiled and said, "Please don't take my cautions in the wrong vein. I'm simply pointing out some of the potential problems. I'm not saying that they are bound to occur. You could move to a city where you'll find a better attorney, a better broker, accountant, even doctor. I'm not trying to be negative."

"But what you're really saying is that if we move, we should only move a short distance away so we can keep our security support and so we won't run into logistical problems?"

"Not even that. I'm only pointing out things you should consider.

It's far better to take these potential problems into consideration before making a move rather than to have them suddenly descend upon you afterward."

Peter and Marge thanked Karen and went back home. They spent several hours discussing the problems she had pointed out and found they were no nearer a conclusion when they started than when they finished. Finally, they decided that what they needed was an orderly method of sorting out their feelings. They needed "pro-con" sheets.

PRO SHEETS (Reasons for moving)*

1. Get cash out of our house and use the up to $100,000 exclusion.

2. Get a smaller home.

3. Get a home with lower taxes.

4. Get a home with less maintenance.

5. Get a home all on one level.

6. Get a home where there were more social activities going on nearby. (Peter said that he really wanted to be close to an area where there were activities, such as tennis, swimming, even card games, that he could participate in when he retired.)

7. _____

8. _____

9. _____

10. _____

11. _____

12. _____

13. _____

14. _____

15. _____

*Perhaps you, the reader, would like to cross off some reasons that don't apply to you and to add some of your own?

16. _____
17. _____
18. _____
19. _____
20. _____

CON SHEET (Reasons for staying in present home)

1. Have wonderful memories.

2. Have friends and neighbors we know and like.

3. Have family close by.

4. Are familiar with all the routes to shopping, banking, etc.

5. Know and trust professionals in the area such as doctor, attorney, broker, banker.

6. Have fairly low payments on our present home.

7. _____
8. _____
9. _____
10. _____
11. _____
12. _____
13. _____
14. _____
15. _____
16. _____
17. _____
18. _____
19. _____
20. _____

Looking over their pro–con sheets, Peter noted that they had the same number of items on each sheet. "It's a draw," he said.

Marge looked thoughtful, then commented, "Perhaps the reason it's a draw is that we really don't know what's out there. You remember that Karen said her function was to give us alternatives." Marge brought out a brochure that Karen had given them. It listed different types of retirement homes from condominiums to mobile home parks. "What we should do is investigate our options. Perhaps then our decision on whether to move will become easier."

FOUR

The Challenge of the Retirement Community

Marge and Peter decided to visit some acquaintances, Helen and Bob, who lived in a retirement community called Sunnyside about 40 miles out of town. They had a small bungalow in the retirement village, which Helen told them had nearly 6,000 residents. It was an enormous complex covering hundreds of acres. "I never realized a retirement community was this big," Marge said.

"They come in all sizes," Helen pointed out, "but mostly large. Sunnyside is actually one of the smaller retirement communities. Those in the South and West, particularly in Florida, Arizona, and California, are frequently much, much larger."

Helen took Marge and Peter on a tour of her home, a modern, two-bedroom unit. One bedroom had been converted to a study for Helen's husband, who happened to be away at the time. "Bob's hobby is stamps, and he's in St. Louis attending a national stamp convention," Helen explained.

In addition, they had a fairly roomy living room and a kitchen with an eating area. That was the entire living space. "Of course," Helen pointed out, "we use the outdoor patio and porch so much that we consider them living area as well."

"But it's so, well, small," Marge blurted out.

Helen took no offense, but instead said, "Perhaps it is small by your standards, but we have no need for more room. Our children are gone, and if they do come to visit, we convert my husband's study back to a bedroom for them. There are just the two of us. We only need one bedroom, one living room, one kitchen, and one eating area. Any more would just be more space to clean."

"But," Peter said, "you don't have a yard."

"Well, of course there are the grass areas all around this building," Helen said, "but they are maintained entirely by the community organization. I do, however, have a garden." Helen took them out onto the patio where there were three very large planter boxes. She pointed out where she was growing tomatoes, corn, lettuce, rhubarb. "By keeping my gardening limited to these planters, I can handle it with a minimum of effort, but it gives me a maximum of production."

Peter nodded in admiration as he thought of his own huge backyard. He asked, "So you only have to maintain your living area and patio. The organization takes care of everything else?"

Helen nodded, then pointed out that although they had their home in an individual building, many of the units were apartment types with three or four units strung together in one building.

Helen then took them on a tour of the facilities. "I have square dancing this afternoon. And this evening I'm playing in a bridge game. Tomorrow there are seven couples getting together for a picnic in front of the recreation building."

Helen took them inside the recreation building. It had a large theatre and half a dozen meeting rooms which Helen noted were used daily by service clubs ranging from Toastmasters to hobby groups. Then she took them to see the art shop. It was a completely outfitted workroom including kilns and wheels for producing pottery. Next to it was a lapidary room with dozens of tools for cutting, polishing, and faceting stones.

"I can't believe all the equipment you have here," Peter said. "Is it all available for your use?"

"It certainly is. Also," Helen pointed out, "the guards you noticed at the gate keep everyone out except those of us who live here and our guests. If you hadn't called earlier and I hadn't given the guard your name, you would never have gotten onto the grounds." Helen added that the community had two other centers, each with different types of facilities, including a library, dance hall, barbecue area, pool room with 15 tables, shuffleboard court, tennis courts, and Ping-Pong tables. "We also have a nine-hole golf course and an Olympic-sized swimming pool."

Helen then took them to see the shopping center, which was just at the edge of the community. She showed them the hospital on the grounds, which had four full-time doctors and a complete nursing staff. "Anyone can use the facilities. Of course, we pay standard rates."

Helen pointed out that although there were broad streets through-out the community, there were few cars. "Many of our residents don't like to drive," she said. "So they've gotten rid of their cars and bought small electric vehicles. They just plug them in at night and drive the short distances they need to go during the day. Inside the gates the speed limits are low, there's little traffic, and the small carts work well."

When they returned to her bungalow, Peter and Marge told Helen how impressed they were with her community. "It must cost you a fortune to live here," Peter said.

"Not really," Helen replied. "My total monthly payment is only $238."

Marge and Peter looked at each other. Finally Marge said, "That doesn't make sense. We're paying almost that much in property taxes and insurance alone. How could you be paying so little?"

Helen smiled and said, "It's the way the place is set up."

STOCK COOPERATIVES

Helen said that the entire village was a stock cooperative. She also mentioned that some communities were organized as condominiums. (See Chapter 5.) When Peter shook his head to show he didn't understand, Helen explained.

"We're stockholders in a corporation. Sunnyside Corporation owns our house, the land it's on, the facilities, everything you've seen. We only own one share of stock in the company, but that share entitles us to this unit."

Peter asked, "Does that mean that you can't sell this home if you want to?"

"No, we can't sell it in the traditional sense because we don't own it in the traditional way," Helen answered. "All we can sell is our one share of stock. However, when we sell our one share of stock, the right to use this bungalow goes with it. So, in a sense, we can sell the property."

Helen told Marge and Peter that she also was a member of the Sunnyside Association. "It's a kind of homeowners' association," she said. "We paid an initiation fee to join, and we continue to contribute about $15 a month. The association oversees the community."

"I still don't understand," Marge said. "Let's say we wanted to buy into this retirement community. How would we make the purchase?"

"Well, this village is fully developed," Helen said. "There are no more new units for sale. If there were you'd buy them from the original developers. Now, however, to buy in you'd have to purchase a resale. But, the procedure is almost identical. Shall we suppose you wanted to buy my unit?"

Marge and Peter nodded.

Helen continued, "To buy my unit, you'd have to purchase the one share of stock I own. The purchase price would be determined simply by supply and demand. The greater the demand for units here, the higher the price. The lower the demand, naturally, the lower the price. Recently prices have been in the $70,000 to $80,000 price range. It would probably cost you about $75,000 to buy my one share of stock."

Peter whistled, "That's expensive stock," he said.

"Yes," Helen admitted. "But, unlike a regular corporation where all you get is a piece of paper, here you actually get a place to live. You in turn can sell that share of stock to others or even leave it to your heirs in a will. It's just as much an investment as if you purchased any other piece of real estate."

Financing

"So what you're saying," Peter continued, "is that we'd put about 20 percent down, say $15,000, and then pay you so much a month on the balance of the $75,000?"

"No," Helen said. "That's not at all what I meant. Of course, it is possible that an owner personally might want to finance the sale of the stock. Some people do, but I wouldn't. In order to buy my share of stock you would have to give me $75,000 in cash."

"You mean you'd want the entire purchase price in cash!" Marge could hardly believe her ears.

"Yes," Helen said. "And there's a good reason. In traditional real estate, it's easy to get financing from a bank or a savings and loan association for 80 percent or more of the purchase price, because you can give the property as collateral.

"But here you can't. The property is owned by the corporation. All you can give as collateral, in theory, is the stock. It's harder and more complex to raise money with stock as collateral than property. For one thing, no one would want to give you a long-term loan. For another, interest rates would be high. But, most important, in the event you didn't pay on a loan, it would be very difficult to legally get the stock away from you. Financing is a big problem here. Nearly everyone pays cash, though in some areas good financing is available."

"Yet," Peter pointed out, "you say that the retirement community is full."

"Yes," Helen continued, "most people sell their old homes, take the money out, and buy this. They use the new $100,000 exclusion the government has. Are you aware of it?"

Marge and Peter nodded that they were. Then Marge said, "One thing still puzzles me. You said that you had a monthly payment of $238. Yet, if you paid cash for your stock, where does that money go?"

"A good question," Helen said. "The Sunnyside Corporation originally built this community using money borrowed under a Federal Housing Administration–insured low-interest-rate loan. There is a huge blanket mortgage covering the entire village. Part of my monthly payment to the corporation goes to pay the interest on that mortgage."

"Part of it also goes toward paying taxes on the community property. And a smaller portion goes toward maintenance, gardening, security, recreational facilities, management, and a minibus service that we have here."

"So what you're saying," Peter commented, "is that your monthly payments are low, but only because you've already paid a huge purchase price in cash."

Helen thought about it for a moment, then said, "I never looked at it that way, but yes, that's true."

Helen then pointed out that before anyone could buy a share, the sale must be approved by the corporation. She said that there were specific criteria that must be met. People who were going to reside in Sunnyside must be at least 52 years old, although, she pointed out, different communities have different age requirements. "Applicants must also pass a physical exam showing that they are capable of caring for themselves, and they must demonstrate that they have enough financial resources to buy in and to maintain the monthly payments. Usually that means showing you have at least four times the monthly payment a month in income (about $12,000 a year in this case) and enough cash in reserve to meet medical or other emergencies. But qualifying isn't really that hard. There are some people in the community who are actually on welfare and who get food stamps.

"There is one last catchall requirement—that a person buying in must be of good moral character. That's supposed to protect us from having criminals or addicts or drunkards buying in, but I suspect that if it were abused it could be used to keep members of certain ethnic, racial, or religious groups out. In a sense we are a closed fraternity."

"Well, I can see that there are serious financial considerations in getting involved in a retirement community," Peter said. "But the fantastic lifestyle you enjoy seems to make it all worthwhile. Imagine, not having to worry about mowing lawns. I could save one day's work every week there alone."

Helen smiled and added, "I like all the activities. There's bridge and sunning by the pool and dancing. . . . We have regular entertainment too. I forgot to mention that we also have a large outdoor theater that's capable of seating 2,000 people. Every weekend we have entertainment by well-known performers, and we get in either free or for a nominal fee."

"It's ideal," Marge said.

"Of course, it's not for everyone," Helen added.

Marge and Peter looked at each other. Then Peter said, "What do you mean? I can't imagine anyone not wanting to live here."

Disadvantages

"There's another side to a retirement village," Helen said. "I like it, of course, but many people don't. Many people come here, live six months, then sell and move. They hate it. I've been watching those people and I think that most of them come from long distances away, particularly the Midwest and the North. One couple I knew were from Chicago. They told me they were on vacation on the beach in Miami listening to a radio report of a snowstorm in Chicago when they decided, on the spot, to move to a retirement community in the sunbelt. They moved here and they hated it. After five months they went back to Chicago. I think that most of those who move here and don't like it have done the same thing—made a spur-of-the-moment decision. They never fully investigated before they moved."

"But, what's there to dislike?" Peter asked. "I still don't understand. Is there something sinister going on around here you haven't mentioned?" he asked facetiously.

Getting to Know People

Helen laughed and said, "No, what you see is what you get. But let me ask you this. Do you like parties?"

Both Marge and Peter nodded.

"Yes, I'm sure you do." Helen said. "But let me qualify that. Would you like going to a party where you knew no one except each other?"

Marge and Peter thought for a moment, and then Peter said, "I suppose it wouldn't be so bad. We'd just have to spend all our time getting to know other people."

"I don't know," Marge said, "I like knowing the people at a party. I can have a good time with old friends. I don't really like spending all that time trying to get to know strangers, most of whom I probably wouldn't like once I got to know them, anyway."

"You've just illustrated the problem with retirement communities," Helen said.

"I'm convinced that there are basically two types of people, at least when it comes to socializing," she continued. "There are those who are gregarious. You seem to typify that, Peter. In a party you'd probably feel right at home going up to perfect strangers, getting to know them, finding out things you had in common with them, and having a good time.

"You, Marge, on the other hand, seem to typify the other type of person. You tend to keep more to yourself. You like your established crowd. You don't tend to go out and mix as much. You probably make friends more slowly.

"Many couples are similar to you two. One is outgoing, the other more restrained at parties."

"But," Peter said, "we're not really talking about parties, are we?"

"No," Helen replied, "of course not. But moving into a retirement community is much like a party. You see, the community is self-contained. On the one hand, that's very nice in the sense that everything you could ever want is right here, but in another sense, it's very bad. Because the community is self-contained, it also tends to be isolated. Those who live here quickly find out they are isolated from their old friends and even from relatives. This is obviously the case of someone who would move to a retirement community in Florida from Chicago. They'd move to a situation where they really didn't know other people.

"But, it's also true when you move into a retirement community that's nearby. Having everything self-contained makes you want to do everything here. Sure, you can go out of the community for your socializing, but then why move into it in the first place?"

"But," Marge said, "everyone's in the same boat. Everyone who moves in must make new friends."

"That's true," Helen said, "but some of us make friends easier and quicker than others. And for those who find it difficult and take longer, it rapidly becomes a hardship. Even if everyone moved in at once, which is not the case, very soon friendships and cliques and other social matches would be established. And those who didn't quickly adapt would feel increasingly on the outside. They would tend to become like wallflowers at a party, islands of loneliness in a sea of good friends."

Peter started to interrupt, but Helen raised her hand. "Don't tell me it wouldn't happen. I've lived here for five years, and I've seen it happen so many times I know it by heart. This wonderful-appearing community can be the loneliest place in the world, if you don't fit in."

"Is there some technique for fitting in?" Marge asked.

"Sure," Helen replied. "You have to go out to the other people. You have to join the different activities that are going on. If you wait to be asked, you'll spend all your days just sitting at home, and for some people that can be harder than it sounds.

"The people I've seen having the hardest time adjusting seem to be the ones that never did anything but work. They went to their jobs every day, and their lives centered around work. Now they've retired, their job is over with, and they just can't figure out what to do. They get up in the morning and get dressed up, the men in suits and ties as if they were going to work. Instead they just go out onto their porches and wait. They wait for lunch, for dinner, and then for the next day when they can do the same thing.

"On the other hand, people who've had a hobby throughout their lives often find this life a blessing. My husband, for example, has collected stamps for 50 years. He organized a stamp club here. He goes to other club meetings and lectures. He loves it, and I have my own hobbies too—my gardening and my pottery. I believe we have the ability to retire to a place such as this, but not everyone else does."

"But," Marge said, "you don't really know whether you have the ability to retire here until you do. And then, in a sense, it's too late."

Moving in Early

"There are ways to adjust," Helen said. She pointed out that the youngest anyone in the retirement community could be was 52 years old. "We have many in their fifties who do take up residence here, but they continue to work for another 10 years or more. By living here and still working they get themselves established in the community. That means when they finally do retire, the shock is much less.

"I've seen others come here and rent units. Our park has half a dozen units always available for rent. The price is very reasonable. Many couples come here and rent for a few months. They try out the lifestyle before they make the total commitment of buying. Many quickly make friends and fit right in. Others, however, realize that it's a mistake and leave, having lost only a month or two in rent."

AGING RETIREMENT COMMUNITIES

"Of course, each park is different and a lot has to do with the age of the park," Helen continued. "As parks get older, so do the people living in them. A new park might have an average age in the late fifties or early sixties. An old park may have an average age in the seventies. That makes a lot of difference in the lifestyle."

"But that doesn't seem right," Marge said. "If you come here in your fifties and make friends, why should the lifestyle change just because you and the park get older?"

"You forget," Helen said, "retirement really has two stages."

Marge nodded as she remembered the second stage, elderly retirement.

"As we get older," Helen continued, "we get less mobile and often require more medical attention. The community here is set up for this. As I mentioned, we have the hospital. We also have complete in-home nursing care available at a fairly reasonable fee. And the paramedics and fire department can reach any unit in just five minutes if there should be an emergency.

"But what I'm getting at is that as we get older and less mobile, and as our health deteriorates, we lose the ability to go out and make friends. For example, take the woman living next door. Two years ago she had a stroke. Up until then she was bustling with activity. She always played cards, helped organize bingo games, worked with the women's auxiliary, arranged parties in the social halls, and on and on.

Now that she's partly paralyzed, she can't do any of that. She has to stay home most of the time. If she wants to go out, someone has to take her and that's inconvenient.

"At first, all her friends from here came to visit, but they wanted to continue their activities and so, slowly, they stopped coming. Now, all she gets is an occasional phone call from one of them. In addition, many of them have their own health and mobility problems.

"On the other hand, if she were living somewhere close to her family, chances are she would get visitors all the time. She has three children and eight grandchildren, but the closest one lives nearly 300 miles away. They do get down to see her once in a while, but the distance makes it inconvenient. I talk with her whenever I can, but she is terribly lonely."

"Why doesn't she move back, then?" Peter said.

"Where to?" Helen asked. "Once you sell your old home, moving back becomes almost impossible. She doesn't want to move in with her children and be a burden to them. And in this second stage of her retirement, she's simply not capable of going out and finding a new home for herself."

"So, what you're saying," Marge pointed out, "is that a retirement community is a mistake for the second stage."

"No, not for everyone. In some cases friends and relatives do come to visit, as much as could be expected anywhere, but in other cases they don't. It's simply an important consideration.

"I would say that the most important thing to remember about a retirement community lifestyle is that you make it what it is. Nobody is going to help you unless you go out, make friends, and join activities."

INVESTMENT POTENTIAL

Marge and Peter thanked Helen for the information. As they were leaving, Peter turned and asked, "One thing we didn't discuss was the money-making aspect of this type of home. In a traditional home the buyer looks for price appreciation. Is that true here?"

Helen thought for a moment, then answered, "I don't know of anyone who buys in here as an investment, but I suppose it is one anyhow. I only paid $50,000 for my stock when I bought this unit. Today, it's worth $75,000, so it certainly goes up. But you must remember that the difficulties of financing and the minimum age requirement severely limit the marketability of any unit."

When they got home, Marge and Peter drew up pro–con sheets for the retirement community.

RETIREMENT COMMUNITY PRO SHEET

1. Low or no maintenance.

2. Great recreational facilities.

3. Self-contained community; you don't have to go far to find anything.

4. Some social meeting or activity always taking place.

5. Small house requiring minimum internal maintenance.

6. Security guards and medical attention readily available.

7. Small monthly payment not likely to escalate, after big initial purchase price. (This is not always the case; see Chapter 5 on condos.)

8. _____

9. _____

10. _____

11. _____

12. _____

13. _____

14. _____

15. _____

16. _____

17. _____

18. _____

19. _____

20. _____

RETIREMENT COMMUNITY CON SHEET

1. Must be gregarious in order to enjoy lifestyle.

2. Some problems in the second stage of retirement.

3. High initial move-in cost (except in condos; see Chapter 5).

4. _____

5. _____

6. _____

7. _____

8. _____

9. _____

10. _____

11. _____

12. _____

13. _____

14. _____

15. _____

16. _____

17. _____

18. _____

19. _____

20. _____

"There are a lot more pros than cons for retirement communities," Peter said.

"Yes," Marge replied, "but the cons are really big ones, particularly for someone like myself who has concerns about mixing with others. I never was that great at making new friends and as I've gotten older, I find it even more difficult."

"I don't know what you're talking about," Peter said, "I never have any trouble making friends."

"We're two different people, dear," Marge said. "Let's look at some other housing alternatives, before we decide this one is for us."

FIVE

Are Condominiums Really an Answer?

Marge and Peter felt that they should definitely check out condominiums. They had friends who lived in one and raved about it.

"Condos" were being built all over the community and it wasn't hard to find models open. They picked a three-story condominium building about 2 miles away. It seemed particularly appealing because it was in a garden setting with tall trees and shaded paths all around it. Peter remarked that it reminded him of a park.

A saleswoman welcomed them and showed them around the models on the third floor. There were one-, two-, and three-bedroom plans available, with one to two bathrooms. Some units had family rooms and dining rooms, and all had washrooms. Some were large, while others were small. "It's quite apparent," Marge said, "that condos come in all shapes and sizes."

"But you haven't seen the best of it," the saleswoman told them. They rode an elevator down to the first floor and walked into an inner courtyard, where they saw a large swimming pool, two tennis courts, and a large barbecue and patio area. "We also have a sauna, a spa, and a playroom where many of the owners have regular card games and social hours. Two of the units in this building are kept fully furnished as rentals. If you have guests coming to visit, you can arrange to rent one of those units. It's much closer and more comfortable than a hotel or motel."

Both Marge and Peter were impressed with the building. Peter asked, "One thing bothers me. This place is so new, yet you have tall trees growing all around. How did you manage to build around the trees?"

"We didn't," the saleswoman answered. "This building is actually 11 years old. Originally it was an apartment building. It's just been converted to condominium usage over the past few months. We anticipate selling all the units here by next year. If you wanted to buy after that, you'd have to purchase from an individual owner instead of the construction company."

The saleswoman took Marge and Peter on the elevator back up to the third floor where the models were located. Marge commented, "It's important to consider that if we bought a condo here, we wouldn't have any stairs to contend with. I noticed that all the units are on the same level, no upstairs or downstairs. And there is this elevator available."

"I don't mind climbing stairs," Peter said.

"You might, as we get older," Marge noted. Peter brushed the comment aside as they went back into the unit that they felt might be most appropriate for them. It was about 1,300 square feet, and had two bedrooms and a formal dining room as well as a small study. They checked out the kitchen appliances, noting that they were all new. "When we converted this building," the saleswoman said, "we put in all new appliances. We felt it would help sales and would also save dealing with complaints about breakdowns later on."

Marge noticed that there was no laundry room, and the saleswoman explained that there were laundry facilities in the basement for all the owners. Five new washers and five new dryers were available at no charge. Peter asked how many units were in the building and was told there were 60. He wondered whether the laundry facilities would be adequate. Finally, Marge asked the price.

The saleswoman said, "The unit you seem to like sells for $95,000. We can arrange financing, if you qualify, for up to 90 percent of the purchase price."

Peter whistled and said, "That's a pretty stiff price for just an apartment."

"This is not an apartment," the saleswoman corrected. "It's a condominium. You will actually own your unit. If it appreciates in price, you will stand to make a profit when you sell in the future."

"Suppose we put down the minimum, or 10 percent, that's about $10,000. What would our payments be on the balance?" he asked.

"Ten percent down is $9,500. That leaves a balance of $85,500 (forgetting about closing costs for the moment). We have a loan commitment currently at 11 percent interest, although it may be higher or lower depending on the market when you actually buy. On a 30-year loan that means your payments would work out to roughly $815 per month."

Peter whistled again. "That's a pretty high payment."

"There is an additional monthly fee of $65 per month which goes to the homeowners' association (HOA). And of course, you would be responsible for your own insurance as well as taxes on your individual unit. My guess is that your total monthly payment will probably work out close to $950 a month on the terms we've indicated."

"My goodness," Marge said. "That's as much as we'd have to pay for a regular house."

"We like to think we're selling regular homes," the saleswoman commented. "Of course," she pointed out, "you could lower your payment by putting more down. If, for example, you were able to pay cash, then your monthly payment would be considerably less than $200."

"I have a question," Peter asked, "What is that homeowners' association you mentioned? Is that optional? Can we *not* join?"

The saleswoman smiled and said, "I'm afraid you must join. You see, while you would own the interior of your own unit all by yourself, the airspace it occupies, so to speak, you would own the building shell, the ground, the pool, the elevator, and so on in common with all the other unit owners. The vehicle that is available for paying exterior costs on the common property, for maintaining and repairing it, and for making decisions affecting the whole building is the homeowners' association. The fee that you pay goes for the costs of upkeep and maintenance on the property."

"You mean," Peter said, "we aren't responsible for anything outside the door of our unit?"

"Not individually," she said. "The homeowners' association takes care of all common areas, and your monthly fee goes to pay for it. That's probably the biggest advantage we offer. People who move in here never have to worry about outside painting, lawn mowing, gardening, landscaping, fixing external plumbing or electrical items, or almost anything you could name that's common to the entire building. We offer an almost maintenance-free lifestyle. Many people buy just for that feature. Where else can you get it? It's great for retired people for whom outside maintenance can be a serious problem, yet who don't want to live in a retirement community.

Marge and Peter thanked the saleswoman and left. While driving home, they compared mental notes. Marge pointed out that the unit really was lovely, all that she wanted in a home. But, although the saleswoman hadn't mentioned it, she noticed that the units were very close together. She was concerned about the possibility of noise, "although I didn't hear any noise in the models."

Peter said he really liked the idea of no upkeep on the property. He did indeed want to get away from mowing lawns. He also liked the recreational facilities, the pool, the sauna, the tennis courts. "But the price is certainly high."

Both Marge and Peter agreed that having a recreation room available as part of the building was an excellent idea. It meant there would be ample opportunity to mix with others and establish new friendships. Yet, they would still be in the city close to relatives and old friends. "It could really be a lot of fun living there," Marge said.

"But," Peter pointed out, "there's often more to these things than meets the eye." They decided to go back and check with Leon.

CONDO DISADVANTAGES

After they told him about the condo, Leon said, "You've apparently noted the major advantages of condo life, so there's no point in repeating them. However, since the thing you seem to like most, Peter, is low maintenance, you should be aware it's a double-edged sword."

Loss of Control

"While many people like the maintenance-free lifestyle of the condominium," Leon said, "You have to understand you're giving up control to get it.

Peter shook his head, "I don't understand what you mean."

"When you want to paint your present house, do you ask anyone besides Marge what color to paint it?" Leon asked.

Peter shook his head.

"In a condominium, not only do you not have control over what color to paint the *outside* of the building, you don't have control over when to paint it. The same applies to landscaping and all other work on the common areas. The responsibilities for the building rest with the homeowners' association. They make all the decisions that you currently make for the exterior of your house. In a condo, only the inside of your home is your castle. The outside belongs to all the owners and you are only one voice among many in trying to control it.

"I can see that would be a problem," Peter said.

"It might be," Leon commented, "but, remember, you're getting a maintenance-free lifestyle in return.

"However, just before you came to see me I was talking with another couple whose home I had sold years before. They bought a condominium conversion about two years ago, and they're unhappy with it."

Noise

"This couple says that in the building they are in," Leon continued, "they are constantly bothered by noise. There are about 70 units in a single two-story structure. Most units have others on two sides. Those on the top floor have another unit directly below. Those on the bottom floor have another unit directly above. That means almost every unit borders on three others. It seems that at least once during the day someone in one of those other units is having a fight or disciplining children or throwing a party or turning the radio up loud or some such thing. They brought the subject up at the homeowners' association meeting, but were told that, after all, the building had originally been designed for apartments. The original builder simply hadn't bothered to put in soundproof walls. Apparently he felt that it wasn't necessary since tenants would be moving in and out all the time anyhow. Now it was, of course, too late. There was nothing that could be done. This couple is so fed up with the noise problem that they've decided to move."

"But," Marge said, "in the unit we were in I didn't notice a sound."

"Were you in a model unit?" Leon asked.

When Marge nodded, Leon pointed out that sometimes developers did not sell the units around the models until the very last. This tended to isolate them and make them relatively noise-free.

"Of course, I'm not saying that all condo conversions are noisy. Far from it. A great deal has to do with construction. Walls can be constructed so that they are almost soundproof. A lot has to do with how much money the builder originally put into the project."

"But," Peter asked, "what if we went to see a brand-new condominium? Would there be any guarantee there that the builders had made a better effort to soundproof the walls?"

"No," Leon said, "there's no guarantee. However, usually a builder designing for condominiums will make more of an effort to soundproof than someone building just for tenants. I think perhaps this whole question of noise is really just a small part of a bigger concern—density."

Density

"Noise often becomes a problem simply because there are too many units placed too close together. The project is too "dense." Other problems that arise from high density are auto fumes from cars parked too close to buildings, and smells from nearby kitchens and bathrooms. The aggravation of always running into neighbors or looking out your window into theirs is one of the biggest problems. A lot of these difficulties can be cured simply by putting fewer units on the same amount of land."

"So you're saying that a three-story condominium might be too dense to be a good buy?" Marge asked.

Leon said that he had seen studies indicating that people begin to complain about congestion when there are more than about eight units per acre. In a three-story condo, considering only the land the building was on, there might be as many as 20 units per acre.

"That's really congested," Peter commented.

"Yes, it is," Leon said, "but again, it's a two-edged sword. Many people are willing to put up with the high density for other reasons. Quite often the bigger condo buildings offer unusual value in terms of location."

HIGH-RISE AND RECREATIONAL CONDOS

Leon went on to point out that the larger condo buildings are usually in the best locations, either close in downtown or at the beach, in the mountains, or in other recreational areas. "Sometimes in excellent downtown areas, the building may be 20 stories tall—a high-rise condo. It's incredibly dense, but people are willing to put up with that to have the location. I'm sure that the builder would have been happy to make the project all on one level, except that close-in land costs so much. It's simply cheaper in such a situation to go up than out. But there are condo designs, of course, that offer far less density."

TOWNHOUSES

"I'll show you a couple of sketches so you can understand what a townhouse is," Leon said. "First, here's a typical condominium design, the kind we've been talking about.

"This illustration shows an individual unit. You can see that what the unit's owner actually buys is an "airspace." The owner has a unit suspended over the earth. Depending on the size of the building, other owners have units above, at the sides, and below. Together, all the owners in common, of course, own the building shell, the land, and other common areas. It tends to be dense.

"Now, compare this townhouse type of ownership: The buildings once again are close together, side by side. But can you see the big difference?"

Peter looked closely at the diagram, then said, "They are all on the same level. There aren't any units above or below each other?"

"That's correct," Leon said. "In a typical townhouse design, in addition to owning an airspace, the owner also gets title to the land directly below the unit and the air above it."

"I can see that's different from the regular condominium design where someone might own the space above or below you," Marge said.

"The advantage," Leon pointed out, "is less density. By not being able to go up or down, the builder is forced to go out. In a typical townhouse design there is less density than in the typical condominium we were speaking of earlier."

"So what you're saying," Peter noted, "is that a townhouse design is better to live in because by its nature it has lower density?"

"A townhouse design," Leon said, "is *usually* less dense. However, in the three-story condominium you were looking at you noted that there were tall trees, paths, and lots of lawn areas outside. It may be that the original builder included a lot of extra land with the project. If that's the case, then even though the units themselves are all crowded together, the overall land area may be large, and that affects density. Often it's a psychological impression of closeness that makes us feel crowded. If we see large, green areas, we may feel much less crowded.

"On the other hand, I've seen townhouse builders who squeezed their units side by side, taking up almost all the available land space. True, they were on one level, but they appeared terribly crowded and congested.

"Ultimately, each project has to be judged on its own merits. While it's generally true that townhouse projects are less dense, it's not categorically true. By the way, the builder of a townhouse may refer to it as a 'PUD.' That's short for 'Planned Unit Development,' the technical name.

"In addition, there are some special concerns you should have in the type of condominium you were looking at."

CONVERSION CONCERNS

"Perhaps I can best explain what I mean by using the analogy of buying a used car. If you are careful and know cars well, you can sometimes get a terrific deal on a used one; but if you're not careful or you're unlucky, you could end up buying a lot of headaches.

"Let's say Shirley has a four-year-old car. Shirley is not really concerned about giving someone else a good deal. She only wants to sell her car for as much as she can get out of it. She's aware that it burns gas and needs a 'valve job.' It also burns oil, and so the rings should be replaced. In fact, the entire engine needs an overhaul, and so does the transmission. Finally, the brakes are worn out.

"Shirley knows that to sell a car with bad brakes could be dangerous. It could kill the new owners and cause her lots of legal trouble, so she fixes the brakes. Then she puts a new coat of paint on the car, fixes up the trim and upholstery, and puts it up for sale. She never mentions a thing about the bad engine and transmission.

"Buyers who know cars discover the problem with Shirley's and don't buy. But eventually someone comes along who doesn't know cars, and Shirley makes a deal.

"Conversions can be something like that. A conversion means taking an old apartment building and converting apartment units into condominium units. Along the way the plumbing, the wiring, and the building structure should be brought up to modern standards. Old air conditioning units should be replaced as should old water heaters. Swimming pools should have new pump and filter systems installed. Perhaps a new roof should be put on the building, in addition to re-painting. All appliances in each unit should be cleaned or replaced. Old elevators should be refurbished. The list could go on endlessly. The older the building is at the time of conversion, the more costly it is to convert in terms of physical renovation.

"Yet, just as in the case of Shirley's car, to many people only the surface changes show. Many people, perhaps most, don't know any more about what parts of a building to check out than they know which parts of a used car to check. And developers are aware of this. Some, who take great pride in their work, spend the money to com-pletely renovate regardless of whether or not it shows. Others, how-ever, simply do a cosmetic job. They just touch up and paint whatever the buyer is likely to spot. The result is that after a short period of ownership the buyers may find that they have to foot large bills, through their homeowners' association, to cover work that should have been done."

"So you're saying that a conversion is a bad buy?" Marge asked.

"Not a bad buy, but a buy to be careful about. I would suggest that you have a building engineer (sometimes called a structural engineer) look over the building and tell you what shape it's really in. Remem-ber, even though you only own your particular unit separately, you own all the common areas with all the other unit owners. When any-thing in the common area needs to be repaired, all the unit owners, including you, are assessed for the cost. While a condominium may promise maintenance-free living, it does not mean you are free from the *costs* of maintenance and repair."

"But," Peter persisted, "assuming the building is in good shape, then are condominiums in general a good buy?"

Leon looked thoughtful. Then he said, "There are at least four items you ought to consider besides density before you choose any condominium."

1. *Price*

"The first is how much it will cost."

"Yes," Peter said, "I was shocked at the price. It certainly did seem high."

"It is high," Leon said. "But, then again, so is all real estate. Many people remember a few years ago when condominiums were cheap. They really were, you know, back in about 1977. At that time you could buy a condo for perhaps 60 percent of the cost of a traditional house on a per-square-foot basis."

"Do you mean that condos used to sell for 60 cents on the dollar?" Marge asked.

Leon smiled and said, "Something like that. If it cost $1 a square foot to buy a traditional home, then it cost only about 60 cents a square foot to buy a condo. The reason was that people just didn't want them. They had a bad name. They were thought of as an inferior type of housing. Then, with the housing shortage in the late 1970s, and the resulting price increase, people suddenly saw the cheapest form of traditional house (on a per-square-foot basis) was a condominium. Prices shot up until today they're just about equal, per square foot, to the traditional house. If you think you'll pay less because it's a condo, you're mistaken. The total cost may in fact be lower, but that will almost always be because the total square feet in the unit are lower."

Marge looked puzzled, so Leon said, "If a house costs $150,000 and has 2,000 square feet, chances are that a condo selling for $75,000 will have only 1,000 square feet. The condo isn't necessarily cheaper. It just costs less because there's less of it, assuming, of course, both the house and the condo are equally well located."

Marge nodded, then said, "But there are all those other advantages—recreational facilities, social activities, no maintenance."

2. Management Headaches

Again Leon looked thoughtful, then said, "While what you're saying is true, I think you may be forgetting several important points. First off, you may have to spend time either as an officer or as a member of a committee in the homeowners' association. It may mean one, two, three, or even more nights a week, without compensation, to run the project."

Marge and Peter looked at each other. "Why would we want to do that?" Peter said. "I'm sure that there are competent people to run the organization."

"I wouldn't be so sure," Leon said. "Remember, if the homeowners' association hires a manager, then all the homeowners are going to have to contribute to pay the manager's salary. Assuming a good manager costs $30,000 a year and there are 100 units, that means each owner will have to pay $300 a year or $25 a month. That's over and above the amounts already being paid to janitors, gardeners, repair people, and so forth. It also doesn't include the cost of garbage cans, utilities, and other materials for maintenance of the common areas. Most homeowners' associations simply feel they can't afford full-time professional help. Consequently, everyone takes a stint at managing."

"That doesn't sound so bad," Peter said.

"Have you ever been in a room with a hundred homeowners, each with different needs, desires, and abilities to pay? It can be like trying to run a three-ring circus. I've seen association meetings where actual fist fights broke out. You'll find that just to protect your own interests you'll want to attend all meetings and serve on the board or one of the committees. I've yet to see a condo where some clown of a unit owner doesn't want to paint the building pink or put a 30-foot wall all around it or construct a helicopter landing pad on the roof. If you're not there to veto the idea, it could just happen."

3. Complex Documents

"Then, of course," Leon continued, "there's the 'Florida' problem."

Marge and Peter looked at each other, and finally Marge asked, "The Florida problem?"

Leon explained it had to do with leasing. During the early and mid-1970s developers, particularly in Florida, built huge condominium projects. Normally in condominiums the builder retains control until nearly all the units are sold. In those condos, however, the builder retained permanent ownership of the recreational facilities, including the swimming pool and tennis courts. The builders explained that they were in a better position to manage these facilities, and that made sense to the homeowners. The builders charged a small fee for their services and leased the facilities to the HOA. That fee, however, was tied to a cost-of-living index.

"That meant," Leon said, "that when inflation hit in a big way in the 1970s, the recreational lease fees that the owners had to pay to the builder skyrocketed. In some cases owners were paying more in the homeowners' association fees than they were in their taxes and mortgages combined! And they couldn't break the leases.

"The problem was so outrageous that eventually state legislation was passed to correct it. Today nearly every state has some form of condominium consumer law. Yet, there still are opportunities for unscrupulous developers to take advantage of unwary buyers. Therefore, you certainly should take all the papers and documents to an attorney *who specializes in condos* before you buy. Buying a condo is far more complicated than buying a house, and unless you really know real estate, you should never do it without a knowledgeable attorney's help."

4. Hidden Fees

"In group ownership, if the building has been open for several years, chances are the HOA fees have pretty well stabilized. Of course, you'll want an attorney or accountant to look at the books of either the corporation or the homeowners' association to see that adequate reserves have been set aside for repairs and emergencies, but chances are when you buy into a used group property, you'll have an excellent idea of what the true group fees are. Usually you can simply ask the seller what his or her association dues are. Yours will be the same.

"Of course, HOA fees can rise and fall. The biggest problem usually comes from brand-new projects or even brand-new conversions. In the past, many developers told prospective buyers that the HOA fees would be low, unrealistically low. Their motive was to sell units. The lower the fees, the more attractive the units would be.

"Once all the units were sold, however, and the homeowners' association started working, they discovered the fees were far too low to cover maintenance, utilities, and other costs. They quickly raised them not only to cover continuing costs, but sometimes to cover deficits which had accumulated from earlier months. I've seen HOA fees which were estimated originally by the contractor at $25 a month jump to over $125 a month in one leap once the HOA took over.

"To prevent this abuse, many states have passed laws requiring a more realistic estimate of homeowners' association dues. Nevertheless, this is another area you'll want your attorney to check out very thoroughly."

"I can see that there are a lot more things to watch out for when buying a condo than when buying a traditional house," Marge said. "But in the end, it all may be worthwhile just to get the lifestyle."

GETTING THE LIFESTYLE YOU PAY FOR

"It may very well be," Leon said, "if you do, in fact, get the lifestyle you anticipate. Unfortunately, not all condos are what they seem to be. For example, do you know whether the unit you saw discourages children?"

Peter said they forgot to ask, but they could check. Leon pointed out that having children meant many more people per unit. It increased the population density. "A condo that has children," he pointed out, "really needs to be much larger than a condo for adults only.

"What about the people who are living there? What ages are they?" Leon asked.

Marge and Peter looked at each other. They didn't know.

"A lot of the lifestyle in a condominium depends on who is living there and what their ages are. Some condos are filled with young singles, and often they have a swinging time. Others are filled with a lot of old fogeys like me, and things move along very slowly. Age is an important factor in the overall makeup of the building population.

"Also," Leon continued, "even without regard to age, some condos have people living in them that I wouldn't want for enemies. It's one thing to have an arrogant, obnoxious neighbor living down the street from you. It's quite another to have her living right next door and sharing ownership with you. Put a couple of people like that in the building, and life there could be most unpleasant."

"But," Marge protested, "how could we possibly know the age and temperament of the other homeowners in the condo? I'm sure that if we ask the saleswoman she won't be able to tell us."

"There are ways," Leon said mysteriously, then laughed.

"I have two suggestions," he said. "First, I suggest that if you're seriously considering buying a condo, because of the shared lifestyle, you definitely contact as many of the owners in the building as possible. Just knock on their doors and strike up a conversation. Tell them you're going to buy in and you'd like to know them. There's nothing to feel embarrassed about. You'd be doing the same thing after you bought anyhow.

"You may learn a great deal just by talking to half a dozen people.

"The other thing I would suggest is to see whether any of the owners have a unit for rent. Many times owners will leave on vacation or will actually only own the unit as an investment and not reside there. Almost all condominiums have one or more units available for renting. If they do, I suggest you rent a unit for a month."

"But if we're going to buy anyway, that would be wasting a month's rent," Marge said.

"It won't be wasted," Leon pointed out. "During that month you'll really get to know the other owners. You'll also get to know the building and something about how well the homeowners' association works. If there's a cranky old sourpuss down the hall, you'll meet him soon enough. If the elevator breaks down every fourth day, you'll learn about it as you walk up three flights of stairs to your unit. If the homeowners' association is in complete disarray with no one able to agree on anything, you'll find out fast enough.

"The one month's rent that you'll pay will be well spent if you learn enough to avoid buying into a bad situation. You wouldn't buy a car without at least taking it for a test drive, would you?"

Peter looked aside. He had, in fact, bought cars without test drives. On one occasion he had regretted it.

Suddenly Marge said, "You know, I have a friend in New York who recently bought into something and I'm sure it wasn't a condo. I think she said it was a co-op."

Leon nodded and said that there was another kind of group ownership besides condominium—the cooperative. (See Chapter 4.)

COOPERATIVES

"Cooperatives used to be virtually the only kind of group ownership available in the United States," Leon said. "They were built up in many areas, but particularly on the East Coast, until about 1970. It was then that new laws allowing condominium ownership were passed in many states. The co-ops became unpopular, for a while, but now people are getting interested in them again.

"One of the most attractive features of some older co-ops today is their location. Frequently they are in the best areas, primarily because they were built years ago before these areas developed."

"So a co-op is just a different word for a condo?" Peter asked.

"In a sense it is like a condo," Leon said, "but the ownership is set up quite differently. Instead of actually buying your individual air space, in a cooperative you frequently buy stock in a corporation. The corporation owns the entire building and controls the stock. By buying in, you become entitled to live in one of the units. You may then pay a sort of rent to the corporation.

"The co-op has certain advantages over a condo. It can regulate who is allowed to buy in. And if an owner is particularly obnoxious, the co-op can sometimes force them out. The control over the project is far greater. Also, where in a condo each owner usually has his or her own separate mortgage, in a co-op there is one blanket mortgage on the entire building. When it's time to fix up the building or make repairs, this single entity makes it easier for the corporation to raise money by refinancing.

"Of course, there are drawbacks. When you want to sell your interest (stock) in a cooperative, you may need to get the corporation's permission. This can sometimes prove difficult since the corporation may want to approve the people you sell to."

"Is living in a co-op better than owning a condo?" Marge asked.

Leon answered, "It really depends on each situation. A lot rides on how well the management handles the building. Sloppy management can mean higher fees. I think in both cases, however, what it comes down to is whether you really want the lifestyle."

Marge and Peter looked at each other, then Peter said, "From what you've said and what we've seen, it appears that condos are a mixed blessing. They have good points as well as bad. There are many features that I like, but there are also some points that aren't so appealing."

"Every type of real estate has pros and cons," Leon said. "There is no one answer. You simply have to check each out until you find one that suits both your tastes and your wallet."

When Marge and Peter left, they decided to make up pro–con sheets for condominiums.

CONDOMINIUM PRO SHEET

1. Maintenance-free (externally).

2. Often good recreational facilities.

3. Good opportunity for socializing.

4. Low price, if you buy a small unit.

5. Excellent locations usually available.

6. Opportunity to find a unit that is all one level, so there are no stairs to climb.

7. _____

8. _____

9. _____

10. _____

11. _____

12. _____

13. _____

14. _____

15. _____

16. _____

17. _____

18. _____

19. _____

20. _____

CONDOMINIUM CON SHEET

1. Loss of control.

2. Units are often no cheaper than traditional homes on a square-foot basis.

3. Noise and density can be problems.

4. Need to pay a HOA fee and to spend time working in the homeowners' association.

5. Need to check out "conversions" to be sure refurbishing wasn't just cosmetic.

6. Complex and difficult-to-understand documents; sometimes hidden fees requiring the attention of a specialized attorney.

7. _____

8. _____

9. _____

10. _____

11. _____

12. _____

13. _____

14. _____

15. _____

16. _____

17. _____

18. _____

19. _____

20. _____

SIX

Seriously Considering a Mobile Home

I think we ought to take a look at a mobile home," Marge suggested.

"That's ridiculous," Peter said. "I can remember when they were called 'gypsy wagons.' I've lived in a solid house all my life and I don't see any reason to move to a lower-class type of home just because we're retiring."

Marge pointed out that mobile homes offered certain obvious advantages to them. They were undoubtedly smaller than their present house, and they surely cost less. "Besides," she concluded, "I'm not so sure they're a step down. I understand they've made considerable improvements in mobile homes in the last few years."

In the end, Peter relented and they went to a mobile home dealer in the area. Both Marge and Peter were astounded by what they saw.

SIZE

They discovered that mobile homes come in almost all sizes from very small units of under 400 square feet to enormous units containing 2,000 or more square feet. (The average traditional home with two baths, three bedrooms, and a family room is often between 1400 and 1800 square feet, by comparison).

The smaller units were called "single wides," which only meant that they were single units wide enough to be moved down a street (usually between 8 and 12 feet wide). Large homes were constructed by attaching several of these single units together. A double wide was two single units together; a triple wide was three units.

Peter commented, "They've sure come a long way since they were pulled down the highway behind a car."

The dealer smiled and pointed out that these new units were designed to be mobile only in the sense that they were transported from the factory where they were built to the site where they would stand on wheels. After that, the wheels were usually removed and for all practical purposes, they became permanent.

Marge was impressed by the interiors. Almost all had richly colored wood paneling, carpeting, large living rooms, family rooms, and dining areas. Many had fireplaces, and a few were even two stories tall. There were choices ranging from single bedrooms all the way to four bedrooms, one had three baths, and most had separate washrooms. In terms of interior variety, there was an almost limitless assortment to choose from.

A salesperson pointed out that they were very reasonably priced. A deluxe, top-of-the-line mobile home only cost about half the price of a traditional home, on a per-square-foot basis.

"Do you mean," Peter asked, "That if I were to buy a 1500-square-foot traditional home for $100,000, I could get a similar 1500-square-foot mobile home for $50,000?"

"Most certainly," the salesperson said, "You probably could get a very nice one for $30,000. Remember, with a mobile home, you're only paying for the house. You're not paying for the land. And in today's market, it's the land that costs so much."

"That raises a good point," Marge said. "We can't buy it and simply live here in your sales lot. Where are we going to put our mobile home?"

The salesperson gave them the addresses of several mobile home parks that had pad space available. Peter and Marge drove to the nearest.

It was a deluxe park. The management kept up all the common areas such as streets and grass areas, and the individual owners were required to maintain their own property. Row after row, they were neat, trim, and definitely residential looking, Peter commented. "But," he pointed out, "it's not the same as traditional houses. No one would ever mistake a mobile home park for a traditional neighborhood. They still all have a certain look-alike appearance. They still look like trailers to me."

Marge pointed out that in many tracts all the homes had equally similar appearances, but Peter maintained that he could always tell a mobile home from a real house. "Look at that clubhouse built by the management, for example," he said. It was a Spanish Mediterranean style with the tile roof facade and stained wood walls. "That clubhouse looks substantial. It's obviously built from the ground up, while there's something tinny about the appearance of these other units."

They went into the clubhouse and the manager showed them the recreation room equipped for table tennis, the two swimming pools, the spa, the gym, and the music room complete with an organ. The manager said, "All the tenants have access to all the facilities. We have 109 pads here and our park isn't all that congested. The tenants have organized a social club, and they have activities every night. Tonight, for example, there's bingo. Last night was poker. Tomorrow we're having a barbeque. We don't allow children in this park, except as your guests for a short while. Most of our tenants are retired people and we like to keep the noise down."

Peter had to admit it sounded idyllic. Finally, he felt he had to comment, "Except that all the units somehow look like trailers."

"Mobile homes," the manager corrected. "These aren't trailers at all, at least not like we used to think of them. It's true that so far most of the designs are somewhat similar in their basic exterior structure. That's necessitated by the need to have the homes narrow enough to be transported on the highways. But the newer homes that are being constructed are breaking the old rules. This clubhouse, for example, would you believe it's actually a mobile home?"

Peter was forced to admit he certainly found that hard to believe.

"It is. It consists of four units placed together. The tile facade and Spanish design on the outside were placed after it was set up. You see, they can do almost anything with mobile homes today!"

Marge and Peter thanked the manager. As they left they discussed mobile homes and parks. There were certain obvious advantages: mobile homes were cheaper than the traditional home, the parks offered great social and recreational amenities, and you could be close enough to the city to keep your old friends and regularly see your relatives.

"And," Peter noted, "if you don't like your neighbors, you can just pick up and move your house like a turtle!"

Marge wondered about that. She said the mobile home seemed to have the advantages of the condo, without the cost. Finally she said that they ought to go back and see Leon. He knew a lot about real estate. She was worried about the investment value of mobile homes.

Leon listened with interest as they described the mobile homes and park they had seen. When they were finished he said, "I suspect what you want is an appraisal of mobile homes from a practical and investment viewpoint. I gather you've already made up your minds in terms of beauty."

Marge and Peter nodded that was what they generally had in mind.

"You're correct in noting the great change that's occurred in mobile home building in the past ten years. The industry has gone through a revolution. That revolution, however, has brought problems as well as benefits for mobile home owners, and you should be aware of both sides of the story."

ADVANTAGES OF MOBILE HOMES

"As you've seen, mobile homes offer a large diversity of styles normally all around a basic design. The builders have embellished the homes with paneling and fine carpeting and unusual lighting to the point where, once you're inside a mobile home, it's hard to discern that you're not really in any other kind of home. This is to their credit."

Price

"Also, there's the matter of price. Consider this analogy. Suppose you wanted to buy a Ford car. You went down to the showroom, and picked out the model you liked. But, instead of driving your new car home, the dealer told you that you'd get your car in about three months.

"You went home. A few days later while you're sitting on your front porch, a large truck drives up and drops a new transmission on your driveway. As you stand there scratching your head another truck pulls up and a rear end is thrown onto your lawn.

"The next day wheels, engine, windows, and other car parts arrive. They sit there until the following week when a crew arrives and begins slowly putting your new car together.

"Now, of course, that's not the way cars are assembled today, but that's how they used to be made before Henry Ford revolutionized the auto industry with his assembly-line techniques. Well, housing today is roughly in the same place that autos were when Henry Ford first came along. Most houses are still 'stick-built' in the United States. That means that they are built from the ground up, essentially one stick at a time. (In Russia, interestingly enough, nearly all homes are assembly-line manufactured.)

"You can imagine the savings in cost that Ford realized when he started building cars on an assembly line. Well, that same savings can be obtained by building houses on an assembly line. That's essentially what a mobile home is, an assembly-line house. Whereas it takes about 6 to 12 weeks to stick-build a home, it only takes about two days to assembly-line–build one. The savings in labor and even in materials (because of mass cutting and ordering) are passed on to the consumer. That's why mobile homes can be produced for about half the square-foot cost of traditional homes."

"They may be produced faster," Peter commented, "but are they made as well? We've heard stories about mobile homes that have been blown to pieces in high winds or that have fallen apart after only a few years of use."

Leon suggested that the only way to answer that concern was to check out the actual building of a mobile home, which he suggested they do after they got through with him.

Low Taxes

"There's another advantage," Leon pointed out. "Whereas a regular home is taxed as real property, since it is basically vehicular in nature like a car, a mobile home is still frequently taxed as personal property. That means that instead of paying property taxes, which usually go up each year as the value of a traditional home appreciates, you only pay a vehicle license fee, which usually goes down (like the license on your car) as the vehicle is presumed to deteriorate."

Good Location

"Finally, there is the matter of the mobile home parks themselves. As you've pointed out, many are outstanding places to live. They are roomy, socially oriented, often filled with people in your own age bracket, clean, and modern, and they have all sorts of recreational facilities."

"Then a mobile home really is an outstanding investment," Marge commented.

"I didn't say that," Leon pointed out. "I was merely giving you the advantages. Like any other kind of home, they have cons as well as pros. In mobile homes, there are some rather big disadvantages.

DISADVANTAGES OF MOBILE HOMES

"Let's begin," Leon said, "in an area that most people are very concerned about, mobile homes as an investment."

Investment Outlook

"When you buy a traditional house, you purchase not only the physical house, but the land it rests on. In a mobile home, on the other hand, usually you only buy the building. You rent the land in a park. What does that mean in terms of investment potential?

"We've all seen how the prices of traditional residential real estate has skyrocketed in recent years. Most buyers, in fact, count on the rapid appreciation when they purchase. They often go in over their heads on payments because they figure that they'll be able to sell at a profit within a year or two.

"Of course, the market has slowed down in some areas, but appreciation is a big factor. I'm sure that most people would think twice about buying a piece of real estate if they thought it would not go up in value."

Both Peter and Marge nodded.

"When a person buys a traditional home, let's consider what actually goes up in value. Is it the house itself, the building? To a certain extent it is. As inflation boosts the cost of new construction, existing construction goes up proportionately. For example, if you bought a house when it cost $50 a square foot to build and now the price is $75 a square foot, you could expect your older house (not the land it's on) to be worth more simply because the cost of construction has gone up."

Obsolescence

"Of course, you couldn't expect it to have gone up by as much as the cost of construction (50 percent) because new homes, like new cars, have new styles. Perhaps when your house was built, a ranch style was popular, but the newer homes are Mediterranean or Cape Cod or whatever. You have to take a certain loss because of style obsolescence.

"Also, new homes have new plumbing, new wiring, new roofs and so forth. Buyers know that and they also know that if they purchase an older home they're going to have to pay for some repair and maintenance, such as when the garbage disposal or dishwasher goes out or when the roof leaks. You're going to lose some of the gain to physical deterioration.

"What I'm getting at is that, considering the house alone, while an older home's value may go up because it costs more to build new today than it did before, the actual increase isn't that much. It certainly isn't enough to explain the enormous price appreciation we've seen in recent years."

Land

"Is it the land, then, that's gone up in value?" Peter asked.

"Yes," Leon continued. "Land values have skyrocketed in over half the major cities around the country mainly because all the readily accessible land close-in has been used up. The cities were built in a series of concentric circles, and each bigger circle was a new suburb. However, by the late 1970s, as I was saying, about half the cities reached the furthest distance it was feasible to go. The increase in gas prices contributed to this in a big way by making commuting not only time-consuming, but also expensive."

"I've heard," Marge said, "that in Los Angeles, the distance from the center of the city to the furthest suburb is about 60 miles, although I understand they measure distance there not by miles, but by minutes. They check to see how many minutes it takes to get from where you live to work and back."

"You can see," Leon said, "how difficult commuting has become in some areas. This means that close-in property values, those vacant lots left for building, soared in value. When they went up, so did the price of existing buildings close in. Eventually, it spread like a wave until the value of land in all areas—even, incredibly enough, that far out—rose dramatically.

"What I'm getting at in my roundabout fashion," Leon smiled, "is that the price appreciation we've seen in recent years in residential real estate has come primarily from an increase in value of land, not from the buildings on the land. I would guess that for every $1 the value of *older* buildings has appreciated, the land they're on has appreciated by $5 or even more.

"Now, to get back to mobile homes. In most cases today, when you buy a mobile home, you only buy the building. You then find a pad and *rent* space. Your only hope of price appreciation in such a situation, therefore, is that the house itself will go up in value, which, as we've just seen, has not happened."

Marge and Peter looked at each other. Finally Peter said, "Are you saying that mobile homes don't go up in value the way other real estate does?"

"Yes, in part," Leon said. "In past years mobile homes not only have not gone up in value, but they have actually depreciated the way a car does. Their value has decreased each year.

"That trend, however, has stopped recently. The newer mobile homes are built to be lived in for 30 years or more. Consequently, their depreciation each year has been minimal. In addition, the cost of building—even building mobile homes—has gone up so rapidly that newer ones cost much more than the older ones. This has tended to keep older mobile home values up, even increasing."

No Land Appreciation

"Nevertheless," Leon continued, "mobile homes have not seen anything like the appreciation of traditional homes and unless there's a big change in the housing industry, I don't think they're going to see it in the future."

"Are you saying," Peter asked, "that mobile homes are a bad investment?"

"Perhaps an example will illustrate my point," Leon said. "I have a good friend, Sally, whom I've known for a dozen years. She had a nice traditional home she was living in, but it was too big for her. She decided to sell and then buy a mobile home and move into it.

"Sally sold her home three years ago for $55,000. She used that money to buy a mobile home for $30,000 in cash and move it onto a pad. She's enjoyed living in the home, more than she did living in her old house, in fact. But let's consider it strictly from a financial viewpoint.

"During those three years, Sally's old home has nearly doubled in value. Today it's worth about $100,000. During those same three years her mobile home has gone up about $5,000 in value. Today it's worth about $35,000.

"Sally isn't unhappy that she moved. She likes where she's living. But she's unhappy about the financial consequences of her actions."

"It still seems strange to me," Peter said, "that there's little appreciation in mobile homes. After all, they don't just hang there in space. They are on the land."

"Quite true," Leon said. "It all depends on whose land they're on. If you own the land the home is on, then there undoubtedly will be appreciation. Some mobile home parks are actually organized as condominiums. Each person not only owns the home but the pad under it. In those cases, the properties have skyrocketed in value right along with houses.

"In other cases people have moved mobile or modular homes onto their own lots and again their values have gone up. It's only when the home is on a pad that you rent that the value of the home to the owner doesn't tend to go up.

"Of course, that isn't to say that there's no price appreciation. Mobile home parks have quadrupled in value in many areas of the country in the past few years. The appreciation for each pad has all gone to the owner of the park, rather than to the owners of the units. Just before I retired I sold a mobile home park for $300,000. I had bought that same park just three years earlier for only $75,000! As a real estate investment, mobile home parks have been almost impossible to beat."

"But," Marge said, "there's another side to this. If all we have to spend is $30,000 or $40,000, for that money we can buy a home outright and live in it for the rest of our lives. Who cares whether or not it appreciates in value? After all, you only get the appreciation when you sell. If you don't intend to sell, it's no loss."

"That's partly true," Leon said. "Some people do get their money out by refinancing (see Chapter 9). But what you're saying is not quite correct in a more important way."

Rent Problems

"I think many people do buy a mobile home with the idea that they can once and for all get over the problem of house payments," Leon said. "When they sell their former home, particularly with the up to $100,000 exclusion, they often have enough money to pay cash for the mobile home. Then, they feel they're free. Unfortunately, that's not the case. If you move to a mobile home park, you have rent to pay."

"But, I've heard that rents are cheap," Marge said.

"Not so," Leon commented. "They are far cheaper, of course, than what you would have to pay if you compared them to the monthly payment on a traditional home. On a traditional home of 1500 square feet in a good area you might expect to pay $750 a month or more, while on a mobile home the rent might only be $200 a month. The problem is that rents go up, sometimes fast."

MOBILE HOME PARK VALUATION

"To understand rents, you first have to understand a simple concept in real estate that has to do with how investors determine the value of investment property. The value is determined by the income. For example, if one property brings in $10,000 a year in income and another brings in $20,000, the second property is valued twice as highly.

"This is formalized using something called a 'gross income multiplier,' which is exceedingly easy to understand. In a mobile home park, all the monthly rents are added together. We'll say there are 100 pads rented out at $100 apiece. The monthly income is $10,000. This is then annualized or multiplied times 12 months. The annual income is $120,000. (A vacancy factor is calculated in, which we'll forget about here.) Finally, to find the value of that mobile home park, the $120,000 is multiplied times a number such as 8 or 11 or 7, called a 'multiplier.' (I'll explain that number in a minute.) If the number is 10, then the value of this park is $1,200,000."

$120,000

$$\frac{\times \quad 10}{\$1,200,000} \quad \text{multiplier}$$

"It's obvious that a big determiner of the park's value is that magical number you came up with," Peter said.

"It's arrived at quite simply. Brokers and investors take a look at recent park sales and compare annual income with prices. It might look like this:

	Income	Price	Ratio of income to price
Park A	50,000	500,000	1/10
Park B	10,000	95,000	1/9.5
Park C	200,000	2,100,000	1/10.5

"Looking at past sales and comparing prices actually paid with annual income, these investors see that in the past, the ratio was about 1 to 10. Out of that they come up with their current multiplier of 10." (Note: The actual multiplier could be any number, but is usually between 8 and 12).

"But," Marge said, "I don't see what this has to do with mobile home park rents."

"I'll show you now," Leon said. "Let's pretend we buy a park using a multiplier of 10 when the annual income was $120,000 ($10,000 monthly). We now own the park and we're getting money back on our investment. But we didn't really buy to make money slowly; we bought to make money quickly. We want to hold the park for a year or two and sell for a big profit. How do we do it?"

Marge and Peter looked at each other, then back to Leon. "How?" Peter asked.

"We raise the annual income. Let me show you:

Annual income	Multipler	Value
120,000	10	1,200,000
130,000	10	1,300,000
140,000	10	1,400,000
150,000	10	1,500,000

"You see," Leon said, "if we raise our annual income by $30,000 (from $120,000 to $150,000), we can raise the value of the park by $300,000 (from 1,200,000 to 1,500,000)."

"I still don't exactly follow," Marge said.

"The way to raise annual income," Leon continued, "is to raise monthly rents. Remember we have a park with 100 units each paying $100 apiece. Let's say the owner raises the rent on each unit by $25. Instead of paying $100, you're now paying $125. It doesn't sound like much of a raise, but let's look at what it does to increase the park's value:

"By raising the cost per unit only $25, the owner has increased the value of the park by $300,000. In this particular park, each time the monthly rent on each unit goes up by $1, the value of the park goes up by $12,000!"

"Boy," Peter said, "if I were the owner, I'd raise the rent by $50."

"Precisely," Leon said. "The incentive to raise rents is enormous, particularly as parks are resold and each new owner seems to make a profit. And that's a big problem for retired tenants on fixed incomes. I've seen prices in these parks start out at $75. Then as the parks are sold and new owners move in, I've seen them go up to $150, $200, even $300 a month over a period of just a few years. (Usually, of course, increases are more gradual.) You can't blame the owners. It's a business for them and they're simply trying to make an honest profit.

"However, for people who bought mobile homes under the misconception that they would be getting out of high rent or mortgage

TABLE 6-1   RAISE IN RENT OF $25 PER UNIT

$25	
× 100	units
$2,500	
× 12	months
$30,000	
× 10	multiplier
$300,000	increase in park's value

payments, the shock of seeing what's happening can be great—and if they're on a fixed income, it can be tragic.

"Of course, it's not all one-sided. Tenants have banded together to form mobile park tenants' organizations and in many areas, particularly California, have successfully fought rent increases. They have held them down, in many cases, to below the rate of inflation. Investigating and seeing how strong the tenant organization is where you buy a mobile home is an important consideration."

"It really doesn't matter, though," Peter said. "You can always just pack up and move if you don't like where you are. That's the beauty of a mobile home."

LACK OF MOBILITY

Leon looked at them thoughtfully, then said, "The name 'mobile' home is actually a misnomer. Consider what you do when you buy one. After the initial cost of the home, there are other costs. Unless it's already included in the price, you have to pay to have the building hauled to the site. An ordinary car won't do for this. A special truck usually has to be used. It can be costly.

"Once at the site a permanent foundation of concrete blocks or poured concrete is usually required. This can cost anywhere from $2,000 to $5,000. Finally, there is the matter of setting up a garden, patio, walkways, and so on. By the time you are done getting this so-called 'mobile' home ready for your occupancy you might have spent between $5,000 and $10,000 above the price of the home."

"But," Marge pointed out, "that's not so bad. After all, the price to begin with is so low. And even if you buy a new traditional house, you might end up spending that much money in landscaping and patios. It doesn't seem unreasonable."

"It's not an unreasonable expense at all," Leon said, "but Peter was just saying how easy it was to pick up and move. I'm pointing out that if you move, you will lose all that money at your first site and have to spend it all over again at the new site, including the cost of hauling the home. What I'm getting at is that these homes are, for practical purposes, not mobile once they've been placed on their site. They're permanent."

"Yes, I see that moving could be expensive," Peter said, "but they are still mobile. You get a vehicle license and don't pay property taxes."

"I'm glad you brought that up," Leon said. "That's another problem or, depending on your viewpoint, advantage with mobile homes."

TAXATION

"Many communities are rather upset with mobile homes. They point out that the tenants benefit from local police and fire protection. In those parks which allow children, the tenants benefit from the public schools. In addition, there are parks and libraries and so on. Finally, there are other community benefits that are somewhat less tangible but nonetheless available, such as clean streets, shopping, and all the things that go into making a community a nice place to live.

"Yet, these same tenants who benefit from these amenities, don't pay any property taxes to help support them."

"But mobile home park owners pay property taxes," Peter interrupted.

"Yes, they do," Leon said, "but only on what they own, which is the land, a clubhouse, and a few cement pads. Their taxes do not include the value of the mobile homes (the most valuable items in the park), since they belong to the tenants.

"To make tenants pay what communities tend to call their 'fair share,' there has been a movement across the country to consider mobile homes 'real' rather than 'personal' property. That means that instead of a vehicle tax, the owner would pay property taxes."

"But it's really a vehicle. How could you say it's a permanent house?" Marge asked.

"In some communities, it's the method of installation. A permanent cement foundation makes it a piece of real property. Other areas have devised an ingenious time test. Their rule is that if the home can be made ready to travel in a set period of time, say 12 hours, then it's a vehicle. If not, it's a home. Getting one of today's huge mobile homes ready for travel in 12 hours is virtually an impossibility in many cases.

"But to get back to what we were saying, not only will rents tend to go up, but owners may be required to pay taxes. That's a big consideration for people on fixed incomes.

"Community resentment has produced at least one other problem. Local government bodies seeing what's happening in terms of taxation with mobile home parks have been reluctant to issue permits for new construction. It's hard to get a mobile home building site approved. This, coupled with the difficulty that exists for other reasons in getting financing for constructing mobile home parks, has meant a shortage of them in many areas. Sometimes it's impossible to find a vacant pad in a mobile home park, even though the mobile homes themselves are readily available."

FINANCING

"Of course," Leon continued, "taxing mobile homes could be a blessing in disguise, if you consider financing. In your case because of the large amount of money you're going to get out of your house, you can easily afford to pay cash for a mobile home, but many families are not so fortunate. They need to finance the home and that has been somewhat difficult.

"While traditional homes have long had relatively low-interest-rate, 30-year loans, mobile homes have had shorter-term financing, often around 15 to 20 years. In addition, the interest rate on those loans has been higher than for conventional real estate loans. All of this means that people who have had to borrow money in order to buy mobile homes have had to make substantially higher monthly payments for the same amount of borrowed money than those who used traditional homes as their collateral.

"This, however, is now changing. Once the mobile home is considered a piece of real property for tax purposes, which as we've seen is occurring more and more often, it is also considered real property in many cases for loan purposes. That means that increasingly it is becoming possible for people to obtain long-term, relatively low interest financing." (For financing details on a mobile home, consult with your banker or savings and loan officer.)

"So what you're saying then," Marge concluded, "is that making mobile homes real property is both an advantage and a disadvantage."

"What I can't understand," Peter said, "is how they can consider giving a 30-year loan on a mobile home. They certainly won't last that long. With the flimsy way they build those things, I'm surprised they last five years."

Leon smiled at Peter and said, "Would you stay they build jet planes in a flimsy way?"

Peter had to confess he certainly wouldn't.

"Well," Leon continued, "they use many of the same techniques in a mobile home. Once again I suggest you check into exactly how they're built."

Peter and Marge thanked Leon and told him they'd probably be back to see him about other types of housing. Then they went back to the dealer. He arranged for them to tour a plant nearby where mobile homes were actually being built.

MOBILE HOME CONSTRUCTION

The plant foreman was cordial, and although he told the couple to wear protective glasses and not wander off into construction areas, he was happy to give them a tour.

The foreman, Harry, said he had been building mobile homes for 30 years and had seen a big change in the industry recently. "Ten years ago," he said, "every builder constructed homes to his or her own standards. Some were well built. Others were junk. But that's all changed.

"In the early 1970s American National Standards Institute (ANSI) rule A119.1 was established which fixed certain minimum requirements in construction for mobile homes. Of course, it tended to be voluntary. But then, in 1974, the government passed the Mobile Home Standards code which was strictly administered by the Department of Housing and Urban Development. Today, not only do we have to meet the federal codes of HUD and ANSI, but also separate codes established by the Federal Housing Administration (FHA). And, as if all that weren't strict enough, since so many of these mobile homes are being considered real property, most of us now have to meet all the local building codes in the jurisdiction in which they're placed—the same codes that a stick-built house meets. When you get one of these mobile homes, you'll know it's passed so many inspections it can just about fly."

"But," Peter noted, looking at a wall 8 feet high and 60 feet long that was being hoisted by a crane on top of a steel frame bed of a mobile home, "they just look so flimsy."

"That's a misconception on your part," Harry said. "In a stick-built home the size of wood, nails to be used, and nearly everything else about the construction is specified in the code. Usually everything is a little bigger and heavier than it needs to be for strength and safety.

That's because of the variation between workers. One person might cut a board straight, another crooked. There might not be a good match, so everything has to be overconstructed to make sure it's strong and safe.

"Here at our plant every truss, every beam, every wall, ceiling, and floor is engineered just the way a car or a plane is engineered. All the cuts are made perfectly, so perfectly that we can use a permanent *glue* in addition to nails to hold our homes together.

"Most of the people in our industry feel our homes are not only safe, but far stronger than traditional homes. Let me ask you this question. Do you think a traditional stick-built home could travel down a typical highway and not fall apart?"

Peter shook his head. He didn't know, but he doubted it could.

"Well, our homes do that every day. Our homes are built to be driven at 55 miles an hour, and if that doesn't speak for their construction, I don't know what does." (Of course, there could be bad apple construction companies in mobile homes as elsewhere.)

Peter and Marge stepped into a mobile home that was partially finished. Marge noted the insulation in the walls and ceiling. Peter felt bounciness in the floor and asked Harry about it.

"That's because right now the trailer bed is being supported on its own wheels. Once it's set up on a permanent site with cement blocks or a concrete foundation underneath it should be as solid as any other house with a raised wood floor."

Peter noticed all the wood paneling and asked why they didn't use more plaster.

"It cracks on the highway," Harry said.

"Are there any problems with paneling?" Peter asked. "I'd heard that there was an odor factor."

Harry looked down, then said, "That had been a problem with some builders. They used paneling which had been made using a formaldehyde base. The formaldehyde gave off a strong odor even after a period of years. Since all the walls and in some cases the ceilings were made of this paneling, the odor in some units was intense. I even hard of some cases where people developed a sensitivity to it and couldn't live in the houses.

"But, in our plant, we've tried to stay away from the formaldehyde paneling and stick with real wood. We haven't had any problems."

Marge noticed that one area in the huge plant was devoted to cabinetmaking. Harry said, "In our factory we make all our own cabinets. We do our own plumbing, electricity, everything."

He then took them outside to see the completed units. They were lined up side by side on an enormous parking lot. "Each double wide is built together as a matched pair. They are trucked to the site separately, but once there, they are lined up. Walls, ceilings, and floors are joined, then carpeting added and some paneling. When they're finished, they're like a single complete house."

Harry pointed out that many features, such as stoves, ovens, refrigerators, lights, colors, paneling, and carpeting, were chosen by the purchaser. He also said that an almost infinite variety of designs could be built.

Marge and Peter thanked him, then went home where they talked it over.

"There's so much to consider that it's hard to know what to do. Perhaps we ought to put together pro–con sheets again."

MOBILE HOME PRO SHEET

1. Low initial price.

2. Great variety in interior designs.

3. Good construction.

4. Great social advantages of mobile home parks.

5. Good recreational advantages in mobile home parks.

6. Mobility. (You can have the home you like moved to wherever you find a mobile home park.)

7. _____

8. _____

9. _____

10. _____

11. _____

12. _____

13. _____

14. _____

15. _____
16. _____
17. _____
18. _____
19. _____
20. _____

MOBILE HOME CON SHEET

1. Probably not as good an investment as traditional real estate (unless you own the land).

2. Big rent increases possible.

3. Property taxes possible.

4. Sometimes poor financing, but getting much better.

5. Difficulty in finding suitable parks.

6. Not really mobile, once placed on the initial site.

7. _____
8. _____
9. _____
10. _____
11. _____
12. _____
13. _____
14. _____
15. _____
16. _____
17. _____
18. _____
19. _____
20. _____

SEVEN

Why Not Rent an Apartment or Buy a Smaller Home?

P erhaps we're going about this all wrong," Marge said. "I remember when my mother retired. She rented a nice two-bedroom apartment in a downtown highrise. She lived there for years. Remember, we used to visit her?"

Peter nodded.

"Why couldn't we do the same thing?" Marge continued. I know that there are apartments available in the best areas. Besides I can think of one huge advantage that apartments have over nearly all the other kinds of places we've considered—maintenance."

Peter looked at her quizzically, "Both condominiums and cooperatives offer a maintenance-free lifestyle," he said. "How does apartment living beat that?"

"Easy," Marge pointed out. "In an apartment not only is the external maintenance taken care of by someone else, but the internal maintenance as well. In a well-run apartment building, every few years the management comes in and paints the walls and carpets the floors. And if the faucet doesn't work, you just call the manager. Then he or she has to fix it. Do you remember Mrs. Green?" Marge asked.

Peter recalled that Marge's mother had a friend by that name.

"Mrs. Green lived in an apartment for years after her husband died, perhaps 15 or 20 years. I still remember the place. She lived in an upstairs unit that was airy and had two bedrooms. The building had a swimming pool that her children used whenever they came to visit. It was close to shopping and was filled with other tenants, mostly women Mrs. Green's age. I'm sure she loved it there. She never had to worry about any maintenance other than cleaning."

"How long ago was that?" Peter asked.

Marge thought back and then said, "It must have been about 10 years since I last saw Mrs. Green. Why do you ask?"

"Oh, just wondering," Peter said. "I know that the real estate market has changed dramatically in the past decade and I'm wondering if apartment living has changed as well. I wonder if it's as real a possibility for us as it was for your friend Mrs. Green."

Marge suggested that they impose on Leon another time to get his viewpoint.

Leon was pleased to see them and asked how they were coming. They said he knew most of what they had seen and then Peter asked him about simply renting an apartment as a place to retire to. "It's such a simple and obvious alternative that we almost didn't consider it. Besides low maintenance, it also offers a low fee to get in. The most I've ever seen a tenant charged is the first and last month's rent plus a cleaning or security deposit. When compared to the tens of thousands of dollars required to *buy* any kind of real estate, you must admit that apartment living looks financially great."

"And," Marge pointed out, "I had a friend, Mrs. Green, who must have lived 15 years in the same apartment and really enjoyed the life. She didn't have to worry about paying taxes or fixing the toilet. I remember her saying that it was the most wonderful home she ever had. She knew the landlord personally, and I can remember their having great conversations."

Leon thought for a moment and then said, "I think it's only fair that I tell you my bias right at the beginning. I don't recommend apartments. I don't think they make economic sense today, if you have any other alternative. That doesn't mean that they won't work for you, but I just want to let you know in advance where I stand so you can take everything I say with a grain of salt."

FINANCIAL ARGUMENTS AGAINST LIVING IN AN APARTMENT

Leon sat back and then continued. "You've noted the advantages, so let's look at the traditional arguments offered for not living in an apartment. In an apartment, you pay your rent each month and that money is gone into the landlord's pocket. You'll never see it again. Compare this with owning property. There, assuming you have a mortgage, you can deduct from your income taxes the amount of your monthly payment that goes to interest. In addition, you can also deduct the amount you pay in property taxes from your federal and usually your state income taxes."

"But," Marge protested, "being retired we won't have that much taxable income. In our position we're not interested in a tax shelter. Therefore, those arguments don't apply to us."

"We will have some taxable income," Peter corrected, "and by owning we will be able to have some tax savings. They may not be as great as when we're still working, but they will probably amount to a certain sum of money."

Leon interrupted. He said, "I was just giving you the traditional arguments every real estate broker uses to try and convince a client to stop renting and start owning. Now, I'm going to give you some reasons that apply basically to the age we're living in.

"I still keep track of the rental market, not from a viewpoint of finding an apartment to rent, but from a viewpoint of knowing what's happening in residential investment property. I've seen rental rates skyrocket in recent years. In some places rents have jumped up $50 every six months."

TENANTS' UNIONS

"But," Peter interjected, "tenants' unions have organized to fight rent increases."

"That's true, they have," Leon said, "and in those areas where they've been successful, rents have been held down to a rate at or lower than the general rate of inflation. But I'm not sure you'd want to live in one of those buildings. Let me explain by going back to our discussion on mobile home parks. Do you recall that I explained then about the gross income multiplier? I said that the value of the park depended on the annual income times an arbitrary number which was derived by comparing the selling prices with the annual incomes of recent sales." (See Chapter 6.)

Both Peter and Marge nodded.

HOW APARTMENT BUILDINGS ARE VALUED

"Well," Leon continued, "that same process is used to arrive at the value of apartment buildings. And, just as in mobile home parks, the higher the monthly rent of each unit, the higher the total value of the building, often by a multiple well over 100. For each dollar a month that the rent of a unit goes up, the value of the building goes up by $100 or more."

"But," Peter said, "you've already agreed that in some areas tenants' organizations have forced city ordinances prohibiting price increases."

TODAY'S APARTMENT BUILDING MARKET

"Yes," Leon said, "but let me continue. Let's go back to the wild days of 1975 to 1980 in the real estate market. Prices of all types of property were skyrocketing. Speculation fever ran high. Seeing the price go up year to year, many investors began projecting that increase decades into the future. They saw phenomenal prices for real estate. Sellers saw it too and they did a strange thing. They began charging part of the future price in the present. Whereas in 1975 a multiplier of 6 or 7 could easily be found by someone wanting to buy an apartment building, by 1979 the demand was so high that a multiplier of 12 or 13 was frequently used.

"Let's see what changing the multiplier from 6 to 12 does for a person buying an apartment building. We'll say the building has 20 units, each rented out currently for $100. The total monthly income is $2,000. The annual income (forgetting about a vacancy factor) is $24,000. At a multiplier of 6 the purchase price is $144,000, but at a multiplier of 12 it becomes $288,000.

"Consider what that means. The income remains the same, but the purchase price has doubled, all because the buyer is speculating on the future value of the building by paying for a higher multiplier.

"Let's further assume that in each case the buyer puts the normal 20 percent down and that taxes are 2 percent of the purchase price."

TABLE 7-2   COMPARISON OF MULTIPLIERS

	Building A	*Building B*
Annual income	$24,000	$24,000
Multiplier	× 6	× 12
Purchase price	$144,000	$288,000

TABLE 7-3

	Building A	Building B
Mortage amount	$124,000	$230,000
Mortgage payments 12% @ 30 years	15,000	28,390
Taxes	2,880	5,760
Total annual payments for mortgage and taxes	18,180	34,150
Annual income	24,000	24,000
Profit or (loss)	$5,820	($10,150)

"As you can see," Leon continued, "with a multiplier of 6 the new owner makes a profit of over $5,000 annually. However, at a multiplier of 12, the owner takes a loss of over $10,000 annually."

"But," Peter interrupted, "why would anyone buy a building that was losing money . . . unless it was a tax shelter?"

TAX SHELTER PROBLEMS

Leon explained, "There is a great tax shelter offered by building B. However, it's important to see that the $10,000 loss I've shown you is not just a loss on paper. It's a loss out of pocket. It's a cash loss. Any tax savings caused by the tax shelter aspect of the building would undoubtedly have to be plowed back in just to make the payments. Even then there still might be a cash loss. In all probability it's going to cost the owner something out of pocket each year just to hang onto the property."

"Then it really doesn't make sense for someone to buy it," Marge said.

"Yes, it does," Leon continued, "if you can count on rents eventually going up. Let's say that the owner figures that within three years the rents can be doubled. Now instead of bringing in $24,000 a year, the building will bring in $48,000 a year. Suddenly there's plenty of money to pay the mortgage and taxes. And look what such an increase does for the building's value:"

TABLE 7-1

	Building B
New annual income	$ 48,000
Multiplier	× 12
Value	$576,000
Less purchase price	288,000
Gross profit	$288,000

"Investors bought these buildings over the past few years in the anticipation of raising rents to break even quickly and get a huge profit."

TENANTS' UNIONS VERSUS BUILDING VALUES

"But," Leon continued, "now enter a tenants' organization that prohibits a landlord from raising rent. Instead of quickly getting out of the red, the landlord can't raise rents and must continue to make horrendous payments without seeing an increase in income. Further, as it becomes apparent to other investors that rent control is here to stay, they shy away from apartment building investments. Suddenly the multiplier drops from 12 to 10, then to 9, on its way back to 6. In horror the investor who bought earlier sees his building losing value, not gaining. His only way out is to raise rents."

"But," Peter objected, "we've already agreed he couldn't do that."

"No, he can't," Leon continued, "not with rent controls. He is usually limited to a small increase each year. But by the same token, in many rent control situations the owner is allowed to raise rents once a tenant leaves. By that I mean the tenant moves out of his own free will and is not evicted."

"How does a landlord get a tenant to move?" Marge asked.

Leon smiled and said, "The landlord just doesn't do maintenance. Painting is not done, carpets aren't fixed, faucets are allowed to drip, swimming pools are drained, garbage is allowed to accumulate. It's usually not carried on to the point where the tenants could raise a big fuss, but it also is usually such a big problem, particularly for retired tenants, that it becomes easier to move than to fight."

"So," Marge said, "what you're getting at is that either apartment rents will go up in the future or chances are we won't want to live in the building."

FINDING AN APARTMENT WITH STABLE RENTS

"That's my own feeling," Leon said. "Of course, I must point out, on the other hand, that there are some apartment buildings which have not been sold in the last few years. These are held by owners who don't want to sell. Since they purchased way back when prices, interest rates, and multipliers were low, they don't need to increase rents to survive. In fact, increasing rents for such owners often only means they are bumped into higher tax brackets. Frequently they are satisfied to just increase rents to meet actual increases in taxes and other costs. In such a building, you often find excellent maintenance and stable rents. Of course, you never know when such an owner might decide to sell out. And if the owner does sell, you can be sure it will be for such a high price that the new owner will want to jack up rents."

"It seems to be a financial risk to rent an apartment today," Marge said. "I didn't realize how much of a risk before. But what if, instead of an apartment, we just bought a small house? Many of our problems with our present home result from the size of the house and the lot. If we got something smaller all around, wouldn't that solve our problems?"

BUYING A SMALLER HOME

"In the past," Leon pointed out, "many people have done just that. I know of a couple, Kathy and Sam, who bought a smaller house years before they retired. They worked on Long Island in New York and they bought a small home in northern Connecticut. While they were working, they paid down the mortgage on this second home. Since it was in a woodsy atmosphere, they used it as a recreation home and took their vacations there. When they finally retired, their second home was nearly paid for and they felt very comfortable in it and in the surrounding environment. By planning well ahead they secured their future retirement house. They didn't even have to sell their old house. They rented it out and used the income to supplement social security and pensions."

"Now, that sounds ideal," Peter said. "I've seen those stories in magazines featuring a retired couple sitting on the front porch of their A-frame overlooking a lake. That's what we should do—plan well ahead."

"It is an interesting idea," Leon continued, "and it has many advantages. By buying now, assuming inflation continues, you can obtain the property at a price far lower than it probably will be in the future. Also, if you can buy while you're still working, you can afford to make substantial mortgage payments. Later on, if the house isn't paid for, as it was in the case of Kathy and Sam, you can sell your older house and pay off the mortgage on the newer one. Either way, by planning ahead you can get a 'dream' retirement home."

"It sounds a bit like a nightmare to me," Marge piped up. "I don't want to be out in the woods. I want to be close in with lots of neighbors around. A lake holds no particular interest for me. I like the idea of a spa and a pool and community activities that we've seen in the other types of housing. It's okay for younger people to be alone out in the woods, but when you retire you want to be close to people, not far away from them."

Peter looked at Marge and then said, "But it's what I want. Think of the fishing I could do . . . and the relaxing."

Leon interrupted, "I've heard it said that only a fool steps into the middle of a family argument, but I think there may be several things you're overlooking, Peter. One of the main reasons, as I recall, that you had for moving from your present home was the maintenance. Didn't you say you didn't like mowing lawns?"

Peter nodded, then said, "But, I wouldn't have lawns in a cabin. It would be wide open, almost wilderness."

"You might not have lawns," Leon continued, "but you would certainly have outside upkeep. And the more traditional the house, the more upkeep there is. I think the point to be made here is that regardless of the size of a house, there is in almost all cases going to be exterior upkeep. Small lots require less than big lots, but very few houses require none at all—unless, of course, you can afford to hire gardeners and painters and so forth to do the work for you.

"Also there's the matter of activities and recreation. There are few locations where a small house will offer the amenities, such as swimming, tennis, and golf, offered by a retirement village or a condominium or even a mobile home park. Did I ever tell you the story of Sam?"

Both Peter and Marge shook their heads.

"Sam was an old and dear friend of mine. When he and his wife finally retired they sold their big house and moved to a small home close in to the city. A grocery store was only a few blocks away, and it was only a five-minute drive to a major shopping center.

"Unfortunately, Sam's wife suddenly got ill. He cared for her for two years and then she died. He was left alone in the small house, mowing the lawns, planting a garden in the back, and occasionally painting. He became very lonely. He had a few relatives, of course, who stopped by occasionally. But the problem was he had this entire house that he really didn't need, yet felt compelled to sit in all day. He had his possessions in his house and felt he had to be there to guard them. His entire social life consisted of sitting home and watching television.

"I'm not saying there's anything wrong with TV. I'm only pointing out that Sam's house owned him and not the other way around. As he got older it effectively isolated him from others. It was easier to close his doors and sit home alone than it was to go out. He often told me that he wished he had the opportunity to meet other people and do other things.

"Eventually his eyesight went bad and he had great difficulty preparing meals. If it wasn't for the public service organization Meals on Wheels (active in many communities) which brought one hot meal to his door each day, he might not have survived those last years in his house. In any event, eventually he had a severe stroke and had to be hospitalized.

"I know my story about Sam is a bit somber, but I wanted to point out the often unforeseen problem that occurs with buying a small retirement house. Often it's not much better than a big retirement house. All that you're saving on is size. Yet you're not getting any of the lifestyle amenities that the other types of housing offer."

"But," Peter asked, "what if you've been used to living in your own house all your life?"

"Yes," Marge added, "and what if you can buy a small house that's near to some friends or relatives? Won't that work out better?"

"As I mentioned earlier," Leon said, "being near people you know and trust is a very important factor. In fact, one of the reasons Sam and his wife selected the house they did was because some cherished old friends lived just down the block, on the other side of the street. But moving to be close to friends can work against you, too. In Sam's case, the friends soon moved. They too were retiring and they opted for a condominium, leaving Sam and his wife by themselves. In addition, the neighborhood changed. The corner grocery store went out of business, and a muffler repair shop opened in its place. And when Sam reached the age of 73 he no longer felt comfortable driving, so he couldn't get to the shopping center that was only a five-minute drive away."

"It sounds like you're trying to talk us out of a small house. Are you against them the way you're against apartments?" Peter asked.

"Not at all," Leon said. "My principle objection to apartments is that in a time of inflation and advancing prices, they can mean financial disaster. A house, on the other hand, offers the same financial advantages that other types of real estate do. Presumably it will go up in value as all real estate goes up. At the same time, assuming you pay cash or get a mortgage whose interest rate does not fluctuate (see Chapter 10), your payments will remain constant.

"I know I may appear to be negative toward a small house, but I'm talking this way to balance your natural bias toward it. Consider yourselves. You've been living in your own single-family, detached house all your lives. You're used to the single-family-home lifestyle. Moving to what you know, while it may not necessarily be best for you, certainly may seem the easiest. If making a choice becomes difficult or confusing, you may simply opt for the easy way out. Since you know single-family homes, you may select one.

"What I'm doing is merely emphasizing the disadvantages. You already know the advantages, so I'm showing you a side of the lifestyle that you probably don't know."

Peter asked one last question. He said, "Is it harder or easier to buy a single-family home than some of the other types of housing we've looked at?"

"It all depends," Leon answered, "on how much cash you have and what payments you can afford. I should point out that at the present time, single-family housing in general is the most expensive type there is. Condos may cost the same on a square-foot basis, but since they tend to have fewer square feet, their absolute cost tends to be lower. Mobile homes tend to be the least expensive.

"It might be helpful if you knew that in general to qualify for a mortgage on a home, a condo, or any other type of real estate, except for a mobile home where special rules often apply, you generally must be earning between three and four times the monthly payment. For example, if the monthly mortgage, taxes, and insurance payment runs $500 per month, you'll need an income between $1,500 and $2,000 to qualify for a new mortgage. That might not be too difficult while you're still working, but once you've retired it may become an impossibility. That's another reason for buying a retirement home long before you actually retire.

Peter and Marge thanked Leon. They thought about making up some pro–con sheets, but Peter said he wasn't really interested in an apartment.

However, you, the reader, may find yourself in a totally different financial position from Peter and Marge and may want to prepare an apartment pro–con sheet. Instead, they prepared one for buying a smaller house.

SMALLER HOUSE PRO SHEET

1. Less maintenance and upkeep.

2. Opportunity to get a choice recreational location.

3. Having the comfort of owning a single-family detached home.

4. Price appreciation like other types of residential real estate.

5. Ease of getting financing. (Lenders know all about houses and are most eager to loan on them.)

6. _____

7. _____

8. _____

9. _____

10. _____

11. _____

12. _____

13. _____

14. _____

15. _____

16. _____

17. _____

18. _____

19. _____

20. _____

SMALLER HOUSE CON SHEET

1. Still must work at maintenance and upkeep.

2. No expanded opportunities for socializing.

3. Potential difficulty in getting easy access to shopping and other necessities.

4. Even the smallest house may be larger than your needs.

5. _____

6. _____

7. _____

8. _____

9. _____

10. _____

11. _____

12. _____

13. _____

14. _____

15. _____

16. _____

17. _____

18. _____

19. _____

20. _____

EIGHT

Choosing a Care Facility as a Retirement Home

O ne thing that bothers me," Marge said, "is that we've never fully considered the 'second stage' of retirement. You know, the period when people tend to become less mobile and may need some outside help or care. Remember, Karen mentioned that at the seminar." (See also Chapter 3.)

Peter nodded, then said, "But we're years away from that stage. You and I are both healthy, strong, and perfectly capable of taking care of ourselves."

"But will we always be this way?" Marge asked. "Isn't it wise to at least examine all the alternatives?"

Peter found he couldn't argue with this, and so they planned a visit to a local retirement hotel. The hotel, called Moorpark Manors, was in a residential area of the city. It had lovely wooded grounds, but as they drove up Peter said, "I don't think this is for us." He was referring to the many elderly people, far older than they, who were sitting on rocking chairs in the front. They parked, went inside, and talked to the administrator, Paul.

Paul welcomed them and then said that before touring his facility, he had best put it in perspective for them. "There are essentially three levels of care facilities. You're now in a middle-level home. But let me start from the lowest level and work up."

Paul explained that the lowest level of care was usually a fairly large apartment building complex. Tenants who lived there, however, had additional services not usually offered in other apartments. This included a cafeteria where they could take their meals and a nurse who was on constant call in case they needed medical treatment. "What the lowest level of care facility provides is the opportunity for the tenant to receive meals and limited nursing care *at his or her option.* Other than this, the arrangement is much the same as any other apartment lifestyle.

"In the second or middle-level care facility, things are a bit different. Here we're organized like a hotel," Paul said. "We've got long corridors and bedrooms with bathrooms off them. Our tenants do not have kitchens in their rooms, and although we do offer private accommodations, most live two or three to a single room."

"It sounds like a hospital," Marge said.

"In a sense it is like a hospital," Paul agreed. "In fact, this building was at one time used as a higher-level hospital. We've converted it to a care facility. I should point out, however, that none of our tenants are 'patients.' What I mean is, in order to live here, people must be well enough to care for themselves physically. That includes getting into bed, dressing, and controlling all bowel and bladder movements. What we supply are all meals and limited around-the-clock nursing. The nurses ensure that our tenants take any medication they may need and also are available for emergencies."

"I'm not quite clear how the first level of care is really different from what you do," Marge said.

"It's a matter, really, of the amount of care involved." Paul explained. In a lower-level facility the meals are optional. Each tenant has a distinct apartment with a kitchen and usually a garage for a car. Essentially, it's just like living independently. The care is just there in case the tenant feels a need for it.

"Here, on the other hand, with no kitchens, no cars driven by tenants, and no separate units, the care is mandatory. Nearly all our tenants could not function by themselves. Although we do have a kitchen available which any of them may use, nearly all find the use of it too difficult to manage. Most of the tenants take their meals at our cafeteria and receive limited medical attention. We are responsible for making their beds and cleaning their rooms in addition to feeding them."

"It sounds like a hotel," Peter observed.

"Exactly," Paul said. "We are sometimes called a retirement hotel."

Marge then asked what the third, or next highest, level of care facility was.

Paul said, "It's a convalescent hospital. It is designed for people who require nursing. In fact, in some areas it is called a 'nursing home.'

People in such facilities most often are victims of strokes. They may be partially paralyzed and have no bowel or bladder control. In addition, they may have illnesses which require special medication or the changing of dressings.''

"That doesn't seem right,'' Paul said. ''I had a friend back in college who broke his leg in several places. He had to be in bed for several months. I remember that he was in a 'nursing home' and he certainly was nowhere near retirement age.''

"Nursing homes,'' Paul said, "accept their patients (by the way, those who live there are called patients, not tenants) on the basis of medical care required, not age. Convalescent hospitals are not simply for those in retirement. They provide 24-hour nursing, often with registered nurses on constant duty. They operate much like a hospital with patients in hospital beds or wheelchairs.

"Perhaps the easiest way to understand them is to realize that the next step after a convalescent hospital is a medical hospital, the sort where people go to have operations.''

"What you're saying,'' Marge clarified, "is that a convalescent hospital or nursing home is really a medical maintenance facility. The patients there don't require intensive medical care.''

"Exactly,'' Paul said. "They are essentially stable. A convalescent hospital provides personal maintenance.''

Paul asked them if they now understand what he meant when he said his was a middle-level retirement home. Peter and Marge nodded, so he took them on a quick tour.

Marge and Peter noted that many of the tenants were in their rooms sleeping or watching television. Others were in small "restaurants" or other meeting places, talking or reading books and newspapers. "It's like an entire miniature community,'' Marge observed. Peter nodded in agreement. He pointed out the beauty shop, barber shop, and 'general store' that were available to the tenants. He also pointed out that the facility provided a minibus service several days a week to take tenants to local shopping centers and recreation areas.

As they were leaving, Peter turned and asked, "By the way, what are the charges for this facility?''

Paul replied that it depended on whether or not the tenant had a private, semiprivate, or three-bed room. Also, rooms with a view of the outside were more. "Our average price right now is about $700 a month. But, remember, that includes meals.''

Peter and Marge thanked him. As they drove off, Marge said, "I think we'd better go back and ask Karen, the woman who originally conducted our preretirement seminar, about these care facilities. Somehow I have the feeling that there's more to them than meets the eye."

Karen was pleased to learn of all the investigating they had done. When they told her how Paul had explained the various levels of care facilities, she nodded in agreement. Karen pointed out, however, that in some areas only the highest levels of care were available. "A lot depends," she said, "on the community you're in. Some communities are well aware of the needs of the elderly and prepare for them. Others are not nearly as progressive and have few or no facilities."

"We were hoping," Marge said, "that you could shed some light on the desirability of these facilities. Thus far all we know is what they are and how they operate. What we want to know is: Should we seriously consider them?"

Karen smiled and said, "Only you can decide that. I take it that you've decided the middle-level facility you saw wasn't for you, at least not for a while."

Marge and Peter smiled and nodded.

"Perhaps I can help you if I explain a little about how many of these facilities operate from a financial standpoint. Let's start with the highest level of nonhospital care, a convalescent hospital or nursing home.

"In a convalescent hospital the costs are, naturally, the highest. Today they typically run between $1,200 and $2,000 per month per patient for a semiprivate room."

Peter whistled and said, "That's really expensive."

"It is and it isn't," Karen said. "When you think that what's being provided is room, board, and 24-hour nursing care for between $30 and $65 per day, it's not that expensive. Many good motels charge that just for one night's stay in a room.

"In fact, one of the great problems with nursing homes is that they don't take in enough money to pay all expenses and make a decent profit. Many are just barely solvent. That's what leads to those incidents of poor care you sometimes read about in the paper. In some homes where the operators don't care about the patients, they skimp on food, bedding, and medical attention in order to make a profit. Sometimes that results in the ill health or even death of the patients. That's why nearly all states have enacted legislation governing the operation of nursing homes. Unfortunately, in some states the rules aren't as strictly enforced as in others."

"But," Peter asked, "if there isn't enough money brought in by the fees, why don't the facilities raise their rates?"

"Most would love to do just that," Karen said, "but they simply can't afford to. The second stage of retirement is often the poorest stage for many people. Patients only have their social security and maybe a pension for income. They can't pay the high cost of the facility. That means that most of the patients are there on welfare. A substantial portion of the federal budget goes to Medicaid, which helps to pay for such patients through state governments.

"Because of the financial situation," Karen said, "finding a good, well-run nursing home is often like looking for the proverbial needle in a haystack."

"Is it the same way for the other levels of care facilities?" Peter asked.

"No," Karen said, "in the middle-level facility such as you saw, the nursing care is minimal. Essentially what they provide is room and board, just like a hotel. Their rates can be far lower, perhaps half of what a nursing home would cost. In addition, some welfare aid is available to tenants.

"At the lowest level, or the apartment with optional meals, the price is not much more than it would be to rent an apartment anywhere else. In both cases, it happens more frequently that the owners are able to operate the facilities at a reasonable profit. That doesn't mean, of course, that there are no abuses."

"I understand," Marge said, "that social welfare programs help pay costs in high-level convalescent hospitals. But what about in middle-level or low-level housing? Are there aid programs available?"

"Yes," Karen answered, "but not as extensively. And this has become increasingly a problem in recent years with apartment rates soaring. It can be very difficult for someone who only has social security, for example, to find an affordable low-level care facility."

"You mean such a person can't get in anywhere?"

"No," Karen said, "but it is a problem. A limited solution has been provided by the federal government. Through the Federal Housing Administration (FHA), incentives are given to builders to develop large subsidized apartment buildings. From the viewpoint of the tenant, it means that the rent is subsidized by the federal government."

SUBSIDIZED APARTMENT BUILDINGS

"You mean," Peter asked, "each month the government sends the tenant a check to cover the rent?"

"Not exactly," Karen replied. "Rather, tenants first have to qualify for the apartment. Usually that only means that they must be over a certain minimum age, often 62, and must have an income somewhat below the median income for a family their size in their area. Once they qualify and find an apartment, their rent is usually no more than about one-fourth their income, up to the actual apartment rental.

"For example, let's say the apartment's normal rent is $500 a month. This is determined on the basis of taxes, mortgage payment, insurance, and profit to the developer. But let's say our tenant is a retired woman whose only income is about $300 per month from social security. Her rent would be about one-fourth of that or about $75 per month. The government would subsidize the developer directly for the other $425 per month."

"Wow," Marge said, "that's quite a subsidy."

"Yes, it is," said Karen. "Particularly since such facilities often provide a nurse on-call in case of emergency, as well as some sort of optional meal plan such as a cafeteria (for which the tenant pays separately)."

"I think we ought to look into that," Peter said. "Think of the money we could save. Are the units nice?"

"Yes, they often are," Karen said. "After all, they must meet minimum government standards. However, I wouldn't plan on moving into one too soon. The demand for them is enormous, but the federal money available for the program is limited. Therefore, in almost all cases there are waiting lists. Typically the facility will build up a waiting list long enough to keep it full for a year or two, and then will stop taking names. In some areas you have to call every week to just keep your name on the waiting list for an apartment that may become available a year or two in the future."

"How do people find out about such housing?" Peter asked.

"It's really quite simple," Karen said. "Nearly every city, county, or township in the country has a housing authority run as part of the city government. Sometimes it is a part of the public welfare department. Other times it is run as a separate organization. Your best bet, since the names of these organizations are so different from region to region, is to simply get out your phone book or dial information asking for 'public housing.' Eventually you'll find someone who knows the location of such units."

"You're painting a pretty grim picture of these care facilities, from a financial viewpoint," Marge said.

"Unfortunately," Karen pointed out, "economically they often are rather grim. Of course, there are other options."

ORGANIZATION CARE FACILITIES

"Many religious and fraternal orders operate care facilities on one or more of the three levels. If you're a member of one of these organizations, you can sometimes get into its facility at little or no cost. Some organizations feel that after you've been a paying member for 30 or more years, they owe it to you to take care of you in your retirement, if you're in need."

"Sounds great," Peter said.

"It often is," Karen said. "Unfortunately, there have been some abuses. The problem arises from the fact that the costs remain high; it's just a matter of who pays the bill. Some unscrupulous organizations, including a few that are religiously oriented, have turned the whole situation around and are actually making money off the facility. I would caution you against these."

"What do you mean?" Marge asked.

"The most flagrant abuses I've seen," Karen said, "come about when the religious or secular organization requires members to donate all their property to the organization as a condition for entry to the care facility. The reasoning goes something like, 'Since we're going to care for you for the rest of your life, you won't have need of any private property. Yet, we can use it to help offset your costs to us.'"

"Sounds reasonable," said Peter.

"Yes, it does," Karen said, "and sometimes it is. It can be abused, however. In a bad situation, typically the member is shown a luxurious room and told he or she will have it after entering the facility. The member is given a sample meal, often of gourmet quality, and is shown gardens and recreational facilities that he or she will be able to enjoy. It may sound terrific.

"Once the individual donates all property to the organization, however, the results may not be as anticipated. The individual may indeed initially move into the facility shown beforehand, but, after a few years or even just months, may be moved out to make room for new members coming in. Some people are moved into spartan facilities that provide far fewer amenities and less care. In some particularly bad cases I've seen, people have been moved out of first-class facilities in their own state into miserable hovels in another state. The poor individuals have already given all property to the organization and thus have no recourse but to go along with the plan. The organization makes money by constantly taking in new members and then giving them minimum care.

"Of course, I'm not saying that this happens in every case or even in most cases, but it has happened frequently enough in the past to make me wary.

"In addition, even if the organization isn't unscrupulous, there's the simple problem of economics and human nature to contend with. If you give up all your property, including your home, other real estate, bank accounts, even furniture and extra clothing, you become economically powerless, or near to it, in our society. What you've done is transfer whatever economic power you had to someone else. It's now within their realm to financially care for and protect you—or abuse you.

"This other person or organization may have the best of intentions at the beginning, but the situation may change. Inflation can make costs soar. You may live longer than anticipated. Eventually there may come a time when the organization financially in charge of you may be faced with lowering your level of care just to keep you on. This person may find that all the property you donated has been spent and the only way to get more money to care for you as well as to keep the facility open, is to bring in new people and new donations. With the best of intentions you may be shifted to a less desirable room, moved from a private bed to a ward, changed from a large airy apartment to a small one out back, and so on.

"What I'm getting at," Karen continued, "is that in general it is a bad idea to give up your financial control to someone else in order to get housing, regardless of how altruistic or high-moraled may be the intentions of the other party. (An exception to this, of course, would be if you became senile or developed other medical problems which made it necessary to transfer financial control of your assets to someone else.)"

"The real question for us, however," Peter said, "is somewhat different. It's whether or not we actually want to become involved with any level of care facility.''

Karen nodded.

"It's really a matter," Marge said, "of whether we're at the first or the second stage of retirement. Care facilities are for the second stage. We're at the first stage, so we don't really need to contend with them.''

"Not now," Karen said. "But you may need to in the future, and there's no reason not to plan ahead. Besides, some people in the first stage of retirement arrange for one of the lowest-level care facilities. That way they can still be active, yet have their housing needs settled for long into the future.''

Marge and Peter thanked Karen for her help.

After they got home they decided to create pro–con sheets for care facilities.

CARE FACILITY PRO SHEET

1. Personal and medical care are available, in addition to housing.

2. Often three levels of care are available to meet specific needs.

3. Some support is available from Medicaid and through subsidized housing by the Federal Housing Administration.

4. _____

5. _____

6. _____

7. _____

8. _____

9. _____

10. _____

11. _____

12. _____

13. _____

14. _____

15. _____

16. _____

17. _____

18. _____

19. _____

20. _____

CARE FACILITY CON SHEET

1. Most care facilities are not really suitable to people in the first stage of retirement.

2. High costs and difficulty in finding suitable facilities.

3. Some abuses.

4. _____

5. _____

6. _____

7. _____

8. _____

9. _____

10. _____

11. _____

12. _____

13. _____

14. _____

15. _____

16. _____

17. _____

18. _____

19. _____

20. _____

NINE

How to Keep Your Old House and Still Get Retirement Money Out

Marge and Peter spread all their pro–con sheets on the floor and sat down in front of them. Then they began going through and weighing one alternative against another. After many discussions lasting several days they decided that a small condominium was best for them. (Of course, it might not be best for you, the reader. The decision to try a particular housing alternative is made on the basis of different personal factors for each of us.)

Once they made their decision, they felt greatly relieved. A big burden had been taken from their shoulders. At last they had a specific direction. One of the first people they told the news to was a neighbor, Darlene.

Darlene was also about to retire. She had a small house down the block. She was, of course, happy for Marge and Peter, but she told them she was taking an entirely different retirement course. After considering the alternatives, she had decided to stay in her present home. Her only problem was that she needed to get some of her equity out to live on. Her only source of income was social security and she needed more money.

She had gone to a mortgage banker and he had told her about three alternative methods of getting her money out while still keeping the house. Darlene had not yet decided which to take.

REFINANCING

One method that had been suggested was that Darlene take out a new mortgage. She still had a small balance of $10,000 left on the existing mortgage on her home. The new mortgage would pay off the old and then take its place. The mortgage banker assured her that she could get a mortgage for at least $60,000. That meant that she would clear $50,000 from her property.

Darlene confided, however, that there were problems. For one thing, if she got the money out, it would mean that she would have monthly payments. The current interest rate was 12 percent. Darlene would have to make payments of about $615 per month for 30 years to pay back the new mortgage. "My income is only $331 a month. How could I possibly pay back over $600 a month? I'd have to use the cash I received from the mortgage to pay it back."

When the mortgage banker realized what her income was, he immediately withdrew the suggestion of a refinance. He pointed out that just to qualify for the new loan he had been suggesting, her income would have to be over $2,000 a month. "The only way you could get it might be for other family members to cosign the papers with you," he said.

"In any event, what would I do with the $50,000?" Darlene had asked. "What I need is income on a monthly basis." The mortgage banker, Philip, pointed out that she might invest the money. "If you stuck it into a wise investment, it might return as much as 15 percent. That would give you as much as $7,500 a year, or $625 a month. It could pay back enough to cover the monthly payment."

"But," Darlene asked, "what good would that do me? If I had to invest it for just enough to pay back the monthly cost of it, I wouldn't be getting out any money for myself. I'd be going to a lot of work for nothing. Not only that, but the money would be tied up in some sort of investment so I couldn't even spend it." Philip had to agree. Then he suggested an annuity mortgage.

ANNUITY MORTGAGE

Philip said that the annuity mortgage (sometimes called a reverse annuity mortgage) was quite new. After a great deal of searching, he had only been able to discover one bank in the area that was offering it. However, he pointed out, this kind of mortgage might work quite well for her. Here too, she would have to qualify for a $60,000 mortgage, and cosigners were often allowed. And, of course, again the property also had to qualify.

"Once the mortgage is granted, however," he pointed out, "you don't actually get the money, not in the same sense as before. What happens is that you only withdraw the money as you need it. For example, let's say that what you really need is not $50,000 in cash, but $300 a month to supplement your social security. Under this type of mortgage, you simply start getting $300 per month. You don't pay anything in. The mortgage company, instead, pays money to you."

Darlene said she had been thrilled about the idea. Here was a way of getting money directly out of her house without selling it and without worrying about huge payments. But, she then added, there had been certain problems.

Philip had pointed out that interest was charged on the money borrowed. In her case, at $300 per month, she'd have taken out $3,600 after the first year, yet her mortgage balance would not be $3,600. It would be that amount *plus* 12 percent interest on the money borrowed. It would be about $4,000.

The next year when she took out another $3,600, she would be paying interest on that amount plus the $4,000 from the first year, so her balance would be closer to $8,500. "At the end of two years, I would only have borrowed, $7,200, but because of the compounding interest, I would owe back $8,500. As it turned out, in my case it was even worse because in order to get this new loan, I had to pay off my existing old $10,000 mortgage. I started out owing $10,000 at 12 percent interest.

"The way it worked out, in just a few years (about 7 in her case), I would have reached my maximum loan amount of $60,000 and then I couldn't borrow any more on my house. At that point I would either have to start paying the loan back, or pay if off. That's the problem with annuity financing. It looks good at first, but it adds up very quickly when you're only taking money out and not putting any in."

Marge and Peter sympathized with Darlene's position. Peter then asked, "Is there no way, then, that you can get money out without this particular problem arising?"

"There is one way," Darlene said, "but I haven't yet found someone who will do it for me. I am thinking of asking my son-in-law, but I hate to do it. Yet I may."

Darlene explained that what she was speaking of was something called a "life estate." It was uncommon here in the United States, but often used in Canada and France.

LIFE ESTATE

Marge asked just what a life estate was. Darlene said it was rather simple, the way Philip, the mortgage banker, had explained it. "Essentially," she said, "the method involves selling your home to someone else but retaining possession of it for as long as you live. The buyer doesn't pay cash, but instead, makes a monthly payment to you during your lifetime. In addition, the buyer takes out fire insurance and pays the taxes on the property. Of course, the minute you die, the property reverts immediately to the buyer and the payments stop."

"It sounds something like gambling," Peter said. "If you live just a short while, it can be a steal for the buyer. On the other hand, if you live a long time, it can be a real bad investment for the buyer."

"No," Darlene said. "The way Philip explained it, the buyer always comes out all right. And so does the seller."

Peter said he didn't understand, so Darlene explained. "First, I should say that the advantages to me of such an arrangement are great. I still get to live in my house and no one takes it away from me. In addition, I get paid a certain amount each month for as long as I live there. The way Philip worked it out, the payment would be $600 a month. It's about the same amount I would have paid out if I had borrowed on the house in a refinance. But, this way instead of the money being paid out by me, it comes back in!"

"Of course, it's not all gravy for me," Darlene said. "I did sell the house. That means that I no longer am able to leave it to my children by will. The minute I die, it goes to someone else. Philip also pointed out that there are other estate and tax considerations, so I should see an attorney before I actually try a life estate.

"There are also advantages for the buyer," Darlene continued. "Besides the chance that I might not live long and the buyer might get the property for very little money, very quickly, there's also the matter of buying without having to put up any cash or down payment. The buyer simply starts making monthly payments. Of course, the buyer does have to be able to make the large payments, but I think my son-in-law could handle it, if he wants to."

"But," Marge asked, "what would happen if he started making the payments and then, after a period of time, stopped? What could you do about that?"

"Philip said there would be several options open to me," Darlene said. "One way of handling it would be for me to deed the property over to the buyer, reserving a life estate for myself. In addition, I could have a contract with the buyer specifying that he or she was to pay me so much a month and if for any reason that payment stopped, the buyer's entire interest in the property would come back to me. Philip said that the disadvantage of such an arrangement would be that I might have to go to court to get my property back if the buyer defaulted. That could take time and cost money.

"Another method of handling the financing," Darlene continued, "would be for the buyer to place an annuity mortgage on his or her interest in the property. That way the buyer would pay me so much a month (at no interest charge), and in the event the buyer failed to pay, the mortgage would be in default and I could foreclose much more quickly and easily. Philip said a good real estate attorney could arrange the best type of security vehicle for me, something that would protect my interests."

"I wonder," Peter said, "if protecting your interests in this case would work against the buyer? For example, if the buyer and everyone else, for that matter, knows that the property can't be touched while you live in it, who will lend the buyer money? What I'm getting at is that one of the big advantages I've always seen in real estate is the power it gives you to borrow money. If you want to get your equity out, you can usually arrange a loan.

"But, in your case, that doesn't seem possible. For example, let's say your son-in-law goes along with this and after 10 years at $600 a month, he's paid you $72,000. Suddenly, he's faced with a financial setback. In theory, he's got a lot of money in your house, and one way to get it out would be to refinance. But who would lend him money if they knew that, in case he didn't pay, they couldn't take the house back, not while you were still alive. He couldn't give good collateral.

"It could even be worse for him," Peter continued. "What if after 10 years of paying, putting out a total of $72,000, he suddenly found that financial reverses made it impossible for him to continue making payments? You could go to court or foreclose and take back his interest in the house. He could lose everything. If he got into trouble in a normal purchase, at least he could sell the house or refinance."

"Well," Darlene said, "Philip pointed out that in theory my son-in-law could sell his interest, if he got into such financial trouble. However, I admit what you're saying is true and he is taking a risk. But then again, he is also gambling on winning. What if I died after only two months? He would get a house worth perhaps $80,000 with only two payments, or $1,200. He'd win big that way, too."

Peter smiled, then said, "I see what you mean. However, you've just brought up another interesting point. Your house is only worth about $80,000. Yet, in 10 years the buyer would have put up nearly that or $72,000. If you live 20 years, which is very likely, the buyer will have paid far more than the value of the house. It just doesn't work out."

"You forget," Darlene said, "about inflation and the price appreciation of homes. Philip said that homes in many areas have been appreciating at the rate of 20 percent or more per year. At even half that rate, or 10 percent a year, in 10 years my home, which is worth $80,000 now, will be worth well over $200,000. It still is a good buy for the buyer because at that point, he or she will only have put $72,000 into the property. Of course, if there should be no inflation, then it would be a problem. But how likely is that to happen?" Darlene asked.

Marge smiled and said, "Not likely. But let me ask you another question. How would you feel knowing that there was someone out there in the world that stood to profit from your death? Wouldn't you be a little bit concerned that this buyer, even if it were your son-in-law, might become a bit anxious to see you expire, particularly if you turned out to be a long-lived person?"

Darlene laughed. "Yes, I suppose that is a consideration. In fact, in many mystery stories in Europe the murderer does have just such an arrangement as a motive for the crime. I suppose it's just a risk I would have to take.

"But seriously," Darlene continued, "this arrangement is so new here in the United States that I doubt I could sell to anyone but a family member. Most buyers would simply shy away because they would be totally unfamiliar with the arrangement. That's why I'm thinking of asking my son-in-law. And maybe, because he knows me, there'll be less of a chance that he'll do me in." She laughed.

Marge and Peter wished Darlene well in her attempts to both hang onto her house and get retirement money out of it. After she left, Peter noted that Darlene's problem was particularly difficult because she was trying to make arrangements *after* her retirement. "Now she only has her social security to live on. If she had made arrangements before she retired, she would have had the income from her job to use as leverage to arrange a variety of kinds of financing," he said. "I suppose it only means that whatever you do for your retirement home, it's best to plan well ahead."

Marge and Peter sold their home and eventually did buy a small condominium where they adapted very well to the lifestyle. They found it offered just the right amount of opportunity to meet others, yet privacy for them. In addition, having already considered the other alternatives, they never felt that they were missing out on something better. They knew both what they had and what others had, and they were satisfied with their choice.

Of course, they had other problems to face. These included deciding (at the time they purchased their condominium) how much money to use as a down payment and how much to hold back. Did a big down payment make more sense than a little one? What should they do with the money they held back to protect it from inflation? And finally, how could they invest the money to give them safety, yet a high return? Essentially their problems come down to one basic question: How does a person or a family handle the sudden appearance of up to $100,000 tax-free? We'll see some answers in the next chapters.

TEN

Is a Bigger Down Payment Better?

O nce you've decided on your retirement home and know that you're going to sell your present home and get up to $100,000 tax-free, the question naturally arises, "How much of my cash should I stick into my new home?"

Before retirement, nearly any investment adviser would give you a pat answer to that question: Stick as little as possible into the home. The higher the mortgage, the more leverage, and the more leverage, the greater the profit when it came time to sell. (We'll discuss this in more detail below.)

At retirement, however, the matter gets more complicated. No longer do you buy with such a heavy interest in investment. Appreciation, of course, remains an important consideration at the "turning point" between working and retiring, but other considerations come into play. Perhaps paramount among these is security. People who are retiring want their future homes to be secure. The reason for this is obvious. Retirement income is almost always lower and less flexible than working income. Recovering from a bad mistake in a house purchase while you're working might take a few years, but it certainly can be done. Recovering from a bad mistake once you're retired may be impossible.

Security, therefore, supersedes potential profit in the minds of most people looking for retirement homes, and this consideration has an important effect on the amount of cash that's put into the home.

The person seeking optimum security may equate that with the paid-off home. In theory, if you don't owe anyone anything on your house, they can't take it away from you. Also, you won't have to worry about monthly payments. Many people feel that at retirement the best way to go is to pay off their property.

That's a most unfortunate belief, as we'll see shortly. My own feeling is that while you don't want high-leveraged real estate at retirement, because of the high payments and higher risk, neither do you want paid-off real estate. Perhaps the easiest way to see why is to consider the case of George and Mary.

George had been a salesman for an automobile tire company for nearly 30 years. Mary had been cashier in a department store. When they retired, they decided that the best housing option for them was a mobile home. The unit they decided upon was deluxe in every way and cost $40,000.

Mary and George had sold their former home and had cleared $50,000, tax-free. They had enough money to pay off the mobile home in cash. Or, if they wanted, they could get a mortgage on it for up to $35,000. The payments on the mortgage at $35,000 were about $360 a month.

They felt that they couldn't afford payments that high once retired since their total retirement income including social security and pensions was only about $1,200 a month, particularly since they figured that they would have to pay about $100 a month for the rent of a pad in a mobile home park.

Mary and George decided that the safest, most secure thing for them to do was to pay cash for the mobile home, which is what they did. That left them with $10,000.

Cash from sale of house	$50,000
Less cost of mobile home (including set-up charges)	40,000
Cash left	$10,000

They moved into their mobile home and stuck the $10,000 into the bank in a long-term insured account. It wold be nice if I could tell you that they lived happily ever after, but that wasn't the case. After 2½ years, Mary became seriously ill. She required medical attention beyond what Medicare and their private insurance was willing to spend. (It is an erroneous notion that Medicare provides complete or even nearly complete medical coverage.)

Part of Mary's care required treatments at a hospital some distance from where they lived. She could be treated as an outpatient; however, that meant that for several months they had to rent an apartment near the hospital. The $10,000 reserve they had went very soon, and George discovered he had to come up with more money, quickly.

The only source of collateral they had was the mobile home. It was still fairly new and, according to a dealer he checked with, had not lost any value. George felt it would be easy to arrange a new loan for half of its value, or $20,000, to cover Mary's medical costs.

But George was mistaken. Every bank he went to told him that the country was in a financial crunch just then. Although they had money to lend on the purchase of new or used mobile homes, they did not have any money to lend on refinances. George simply could not get a loan. (Note: A financial crunch such as this occurred in 1979–1980, as well as many times before. It is not as rare as many people would like to believe.) George was told that if he'd wait just six months, money conditions would change and they could fund the loan.

However, George had hospital and doctor bills to pay, and he could not wait. He went to the public welfare department to apply for aid. Again, he was turned down. He owned a mobile home worth $40,000. He wouldn't be given welfare while he had such a valuable piece of property. Since he didn't have friends or relatives from whom he could borrow, George's final alternative was to sell the mobile home, which he did for $45,000 in cash.

He used the $20,000 to pay off Mary's additional medical expenses, and then, with the remaining $25,000, they went looking for a new home.

This is not a fictional story, although the names have been changed. I used it here to illustrate that the notion that paying off your home makes it more secure is false. Just the opposite may, in fact, be true. It certainly was in the case of George and Mary.

Let's go back. When they first bought their mobile home, they learned that the maximum loan they could get would be $35,000, with a down payment of $5,000. They could not afford the payments on such a big loan. However, they could have afforded to finance a lower loan. Borrowing $20,000 at the time of the purchase (assuming a 20-year loan at 12 percent interest) would have only cost them about $220 a month, a figure they probably could well have handled. The extra $20,000 they could then have kept in the bank or elsewhere until an emergency arose. The money would have been ready when needed.

The point is that borrowing money on real estate is almost always *easiest* at the time of purchase. Once you own the property, it can become very difficult to borrow on it. Therefore, it's best to plan ahead. It may be wisest to consider a mortgage that you can afford at the time of purchase, rather than paying cash.

This has other advantages. When we're working, we really have very little time for looking into areas where we might be able to make money by spending money. By this I mean modest, low-risk investments. But, once we're retired, the opportunity for such investments may present themselves. In George and Mary's case it was a medical emergency, but in other cases investment opportunities may arise. For example, you might get a chance to go in with a friend or relative on a short-term stock or business investment. If the money is available, you can make the investment.

LIQUIDITY

The problem we're considering here is really one of "liquidity." In financing that simply means how fluid your cash position is, how quickly you can convert an asset to cash. Real estate is possibly the least fluid of any investment. Traditionally, real estate has been nonliquid, and people who invest in it are usually cautioned that they shouldn't expect to get their money out in less than about three years.

The same holds true for buying a home as for buying a real estate investment. As we've seen with George and Mary, liquidity can be a big problem.

But how big of a mortgage should you get?

George and Mary felt that to go for the maximum, with payments of about $360 a month with a $1,200 a month income was just too high. But how does one determine the just right amount of mortgage on a piece of property?

I've found that asking, "How big a mortgage?" is the same as asking, "How big a liquid reserve should you have?" Very few can give specific answers to this question. One couple, such as we've seen, may say that $10,000 in the bank is enough. Another may feel uncomfortable with anything less than $100,000. Most people say that they want enough for emergencies or to invest with or just because it makes them feel good "to have money in the bank." These reasons, however, don't lead us to specific amounts of money.

"HOW BIG A MORTGAGE" REALLY MEANS "HOW BIG A MONTHLY PAYMENT"

On the other hand, if you ask a person how big a monthly payment he or she can afford, you usually get an answer down to the dollar. People usually know exactly what they can afford in terms of monthly payments.

I think the reason for this is that, for nearly all our working lives, most of us deal with paychecks. Our "wealth" comes to us in the form of weekly or monthly increments. After 30 or 40 years of dealing with so much money per month, we get pretty good at it.

Suddenly, at retirement, the tables are turned. All of a sudden we get a single large payment in cash, up to $100,000 tax-free. Chances are that most of us have never had to deal with a sum of money that size before in our lives. We are totally unprepared to handle it. We really don't know how much we should keep back and how much we should stick in our home.

That's why it's best to stick with the monthly payment approach. It's something we're familiar with, something we can handle. It can lead us to a decision on how big a down payment to make.

How big a monthly mortgage payment can you afford *after retirement?* Or, after expenses, how much of your income is left for mortgage payments?

DETERMINING WHAT MORTGAGE PAYMENT YOU CAN AFFORD AFTER RETIREMENT

If you've already retired, I'm sure you'll have the answer to that on the tip of your tongue. If you haven't yet retired, however, the answer may be a bit more difficult. The reason is that chances are you'll be living on a smaller income than before and you won't yet know what your expenses are.

If that's the case, then I suggest something which can prove to be very helpful—a trial retirement. This is a three- to six-month period during which you take time off work and act as if you're retired. It may be in the form of accumulated vacation time, or a leave of absence, or simply as a period between jobs. The point is that you have the opportunity to get your feet wet and try the water, before you jump. It can save a lot of pain and anguish later on. It can show you what your real retirement expenses will be.

FINDING YOUR SECOND HALF EXPENSES

I've heard many people argue that the second half is, in fact, different. Money is less of a problem. The reason is that less money is required to live on. The expense of buying work clothes, for example, whether you were a white- or a blue-collar worker, is eliminated. So is the expense of driving to and from work. In retirement one simply doesn't need as much money as before.

That's not what I found.

After a relatively short period of adjustment, retirement can be just as expensive as working, if not more expensive!

Good friends of mine, Jerry and Judy, took a trial retirement while I was writing this book. I observed them closely. They saved on not having to buy work clothes, not having to drive to work, not having as many auto repair expenses, and so on. Yet, they were shocked to see their monthly expenses. Jerry and I kept a record, and Table 10-1 shows how it looked. Mortgage payments are not included.

Jerry and Judy were spending $73 a month more during their trial retirement than before! But just how realistic are these figures? The only way to find out is to look at them a bit more closely.

Property taxes: Jerry's taxes of $100 a month were already quite low because he lived in California. In most other parts of the country, the rate would be much higher.

Fire and theft: Whether you own or rent, some form of casualty insurance is a necessity. The amounts here are not particularly high.

Health insurance: It's not generally known that most retirees have to pay something for health insurance, even if they qualify for Medicare! The Medicare program does pay a great deal, but its administration is complex and often confused, and typically it will not pay a sub-

TABLE 10-1 JERRY AND JUDY'S EXPENSES

	Preretirement	*Postretirement*
Property taxes (monthly)	$ 100	$ 100
Insurance (monthly)		
Fire and theft	24	26
Health	-0-*	75 (private plan)
Clothes	150	50
Gasoline	150	150
Utilities and phone	130	136
Food	250	280
Entertainment	150	210
Gifts and miscellaneous	46	46
Emergencies†	250	250
	$1150	$1223

*Covered in work policy.

†Emergencies include fixing the washer, the dryer, the TV, the car, the sink, or our own bodies (to cover that portion of medical costs not covered by health insurance).

stantial portion of many bills. (It won't pay 20 percent or more of many costs.) Private insurance, therefore, is a requirement, and it is even more necessary if you don't yet qualify for Medicare.

Clothes: Retired people need less money for clothes, but they don't eliminate their need for clothes altogether.

Gasoline: This item may have been the most surprising. Jerry and Judy's gasoline bills stayed about the same. I believe the reason is that with more leisure time, they tended to drive more places. They spent more time going to the beach, to visit relatives and friends, and on vacation. (Also, gas prices went up.)

Utilities and telephone: Phone bills went down, but utilities increased as the rising cost of energy was passed on by the utility companies.

Food: They had to eat, and food prices certainly weren't going down.

Entertainment: In order to have fun with all that time off, Jerry and Judy found they wanted to do more things. They saw more movies, went to more plays, and ate out more often, and it all cost more.

Gifts and miscellaneous: No reduction here.

Emergencies: Everyone has emergencies all the time. If one doesn't occur this month, two will occur next month. Technically speaking, this is a category that an accountant might term "reserve for repairs, replacement, and maintenance," All the *things* we have wear out. It costs money to keep them going, fix them, or replace them. The amount here was not unrealistic for Jerry and Judy (and probably not unrealistic, in proportion to your income, for you).

The result was an increase in their expenses during the trial retirement.

At this point I feel sure I can hear several readers saying, "But they surely were extravagant. They could have cut back in so many areas. They didn't have to go driving all around. They could have spent less on entertainment, gifts, even food. There must easily be $250 worth of fat, maybe more, in the second budget."

True. But what's important to see here is that Jerry and Judy's retirement budget allowed them to have a lifestyle they wanted. This included taking more trips to visit relatives, friends, and parts of the country they wanted to see. It included eating out more often and spending more money on entertainment.

Certainly, they could have cut back, but that would have meant denying the very lifestyle they wanted. Consider the areas where they could have cut back most easily: transportation, food, and entertainment—all areas which directly affect lifestyle. To spend less would have meant giving up the various items that they most looked forward to.

PUTTING EXPENSES AND INCOME TOGETHER TO FIND THE MONTHLY PAYMENT

In any event, they found that their retirement budget was higher by $73 a month than their working budget. There was, of course, a difference that wasn't mentioned. When working they were making a mortgage payment of $750 a month. That payment upon retirement, assuming they had the cash from their house to use to purchase another house, could be entirely eliminated if they wanted. The real question came back to, "How big a mortgage can we afford?" They now had the tools to find the answer.

They knew that their income during retirement would be $1,500 per month, including social security and income generated from several real estate investments they had made.

Retirement income	$1,500
Less expenses	1,223
Income available for mortage payment	$ 277

Jerry and Judy had $277 available from their income to use toward a mortgage. How big a mortgage would that yield? Assuming they got a 30-year loan and the interest rate charged them was 12 percent, they could afford a mortgage of about $27,000. (We'll go into how this was determined in just a few moments.)

Working backward from expenses and known income, Jerry and Judy were very quickly able to pinpoint exactly how big a mortgage they could afford. That made it fairly simply to determine how much cash they should put down on their retirement home. They simply subtracted the mortgage amount from the price. If they were buying a $80,000 condo, that meant putting down $53,000.

Price	$80,000
Less mortgage	27,000
Down payment	$53,000

Of course, things often don't work out as neatly as shown here. Jerry and Judy might not have had $53,000 (plus closing costs) to put down on the condo. They might have been forced to try to get a bigger mortgage and cut back on other expenses. Or their retirement income, $1,500 per month, might not have been so high. The point, however, is that once you know your own monthly income and expenses, you can quickly figure out how much of a down payment you can comfortably afford to make. (We'll get into whether or not you should make it at the end of this chapter.)

Now, let's go back to that calculation that Jerry and Judy made once they found out how big a mortgage payment they could afford. How did they get from knowing they could afford to pay $277 a month to the knowledge that this translated into a $27,000 mortgage? (Those readers who already know how this is done may feel free to skip the next section.)

CALCULATING THE DOWN PAYMENT ONCE YOU KNOW THE MONTHLY PAYMENT

The way to translate monthly payment into mortgage amount involves making a small purchase. You have to go to your local bookstore and buy an "amortization table." These are readily available. (Some banks and savings and loan associations give them out free to customers.)

"Amortization" means paying off a mortgage in equal installments (no balloon payments or no one installment bigger than any others). Amortization tables are usually organized by interest rate. Each section is for a different rate of interest: 11 percent, 11¼ percent, 11½ percent, 12 percent, and so forth. The tables are also organized by term, or the number of years the mortgage is to run, as well as by the mortgage amount. A typical section in an amortization book might look something like Table 10-2.

This is the section for 12 percent interest. An amortization book, of course, would include amounts of mortgage below $10,000 and above $20,000—usually up to $100,000. In addition, besides just giving the term for 15 years and 30 years, it would also give in-between terms.

Using this table is the essence of simplicity. Let's say you want to get a $15,000 mortgage for 30 years. What will your payments be? You simply go down the left-hand column to $15,000, then read across to the 30-year column. Instantly you see that to fully pay back the mortgage (including interest) would cost you $154.29 a month.

Once you know your maximum monthly payment, using the chart

**TABLE 10-2   AMORTIZATION CHART FOR 12
PERCENT INTEREST RATE**

Mortgage Amount	Monthly payment at:	
	15 years	*30 years*
$10,000	120.02	102.86
11,000	132.02	113.15
12,000	144.03	123.44
13,000	156.03	133.72
14,000	168.03	144.01
15,000	180.03	154.29
16,000	192.04	164.58
17,000	204.04	174.87
18,000	216.04	185.15
19,000	228.04	195.44
20,000	240.04	205.73

to find out how big a mortgage you can afford is nearly as simple. There are, however, a few steps in between. First, you must determine the current mortgage interest rate. You can find this out by calling up several savings and loan associations in your area. Once you get a loan officer on the phone, you simply ask, "What's the mortgage rate for . . . ?" Here you list the kind of home you're buying. Traditional houses, condominiums, and some retirement communities tend to have one rate. Mobile homes, in some areas of the country where they are still considered vehicular rather than real property, tend to have a rate a percentage point or two higher. The officer will give you the rate at the time you call. We'll assume it's 12 percent.

Next, you ask the officer the maximum term. (In real estate it usually makes sense to go for the longest term. This gives you the lowest payment.) Again, for traditional homes, condominiums, and some retirement community homes, the maximum term is usually 30 years (or sometimes 29½ years). For mobile homes it's frequently only about 15 years.

Now you have all the information you need to find your maximum loan amount. You simply turn to the section of your amortization book that lists 12 percent loans. Then you go to the column for 30 years (assuming you're not buying a mobile home) and read down the column until you find the mortgage payment you can afford. We'll assume you've decided you can afford monthly mortgage payments of $200 per month. Reading down the right-hand column, we come to 195.44 and 205.73. $200 per month will be somewhere in between, so you can assume the maximum mortgage you can afford will be about $19,500.

LENDERS' REQUIREMENTS

Now you know how to calculate how much money you can afford to pay on a mortgage, the mortgage amount, and indirectly, what we really started out to find, the maximum affordable down payment. Before we discuss whether or not you should now try to get that mortgage, let's consider one other possible obstacle, the lender.

Deciding how big a mortgage you can afford is one thing, but getting it may be quite another. Lenders have strict requirements regarding mortgage amounts. They can be summarized in terms of four basic considerations; appraised value, buyer's income, buyer's credit, and availability of money. Let's take them one at a time.

Appraised Value

Lenders give mortgages (or trust deeds—a slightly different kind of security device coming into increasing popularity) on the basis, in part, of collateral. The collateral is the property. It only stands to reason that no lender will loan out more than the property is worth. To do so would be financial suicide. The borrower could take the money and not make payments. The lender's primary recourse would be to take back the property which, if it were worth less than the loan, would net the lender out with a loss. Therefore, lenders tend to loan money at less than the value of the property. That way, should they be forced to take the property back, they could quickly sell it at a reduced rate and still come out not losing money. (In recent years, they've made money on foreclosure sales.)

Most lenders are precluded by federal or state law from making real estate loans for more than 80 percent of their appraisal of a property's value on uninsured loans. (In some cases this amount can be 90 percent.) Quite simply the lender, usually a savings and loan association, will go out and determine the market value of the property. This becomes its "appraised value." The lender will then usually loan 80 percent of this amount. In some cases, where private insurance of the mortgage is obtained, the lender can loan up to 95 percent of appraised value. In other cases, where the loan is insured by the Federal Housing Administration, the loan amount can go as high as about 97 percent. When the loan is guaranteed by the Veteran's Administration, the loan amount can be 100 percent. (In both the last two cases, the FHA and the VA examine the property themselves and make their own appraised values.)

Regardless of how much money you may want to borrow on a piece of property, under normal circumstances you will not be able to borrow more than the amounts indicated above.

Buyer's Income

Lenders need some assurance that the borrower can repay the mortgage money loaned out. The best form of assurance is that the borrower has an income high enough to make the monthly mortgage payment as well as meet all other obligations. Over the years a formula has been worked out to determine the buyer's income. In today's market that formula says that the buyer must be making at least 3 to 3½ times the mortgage payment in order to qualify for the loan.

What this means is that if the mortgage amount is $200, as in our last example, the borrower must be making 3 to 3½ times that amount or between $600 and $700 per month. This income figure is before taxes, but after *any* other long-term payments. For example, a borrower who made $600 per month and was paying $50 a month on a three-year car loan would not qualify for the mortgage, because the borrower's net income would only be $550 per month.

These "qualifying" rules are strict. For mortgages higher than 80 percent, such as those which have private insurance or FHA insurance, the rule is generally that the borrower must be making closer to four times the monthly payment. In this case that would be a minimum of $800 a month. It's harder to get these kinds of loans for this reason.

GI loans also have higher requirements, except that the borrower can appeal directly to the Veteran's Administration. If you can show ability to meet the payments regardless of income, it may be possible to qualify for the loan. Check with your local Veteran's Administration home guarantee program.

Buyer's Credit

In all cases the buyer must show that he or she is a good credit risk. This is done in two ways. The first way is by a credit check. The lender has a credit bureau check on the credit history of the borrower. This history usually shows not only any accounts not paid or paid slowly, but accounts paid on time.

A big mistake some people make is believing that because they've never borrowed anything, they have a good credit history. A person who's never borrowed has no credit history and will find it virtually impossible to get a mortgage. The best credit risk is a borrower who can show repeated borrowing from a variety of sources, including banks, and repeated paying back on time. Even one default can cause a lender to question giving a mortgage. A history of defaults on loans or of late payments will surely result in a rejection by the lender. In the case of privately insured loans, FHA-insured loans, and GI loans, the credit requirements are usually most strict.

Availability of Money

After examining all these requirements for getting real estate financing, you may think that it's computer precise. Plug in the required infor-mation and out pops the money. However, that's not the case. A lot depends on the availability of money.

When money is tight (scarce) and lenders have little to loan out, they adhere strictly to these rules and may even make them stricter. Their reasoning is easy to understand. There are far more people try-ing to get mortgages than there is money to loan. Why shouldn't they only consider the most qualified buyers?

On the other hand, when money is loose (plentiful), lenders are in the opposite position. They may be filled with funds on which they're paying interest, and yet few people may be borrowing. In such circum-stances they'll often liberalize the qualifications, sometimes to a sur-prising degree.

SHOULD YOU GO FOR THE BIGGER MORTGAGE AND THE SMALLER DOWN PAYMENT?

After all that's been said, you probably have a good idea of how big a mortgage you can afford, or at least you know how to find out. Perhaps now, however, you're still concerned about the wisdom of taking out a mortgage. I've heard people say, "If I borrow $20,000 I'm afraid I'll just piddle it away foolishly. I'll probably buy a new car or a boat or something I really don't need. Whereas, if I keep the money in the house, then because it is so difficult to get to, I'll have to think twice before I spend it foolishly."

A concern such as this is wisely taken. Each of us knows ourselves best. If we are the sort to foolishly spend whatever money we get in our hands, then perhaps leaving it in the house is the best method. However, most people I've talked with who have retired are quite the opposite. They've gotten past their free-spending days and are vitally concerned about the future. They are certainly not about to throw money away. In fact, I've heard comments such as, "I prefer to get the mortgage because then I won't waste the monthly payment! If I had an extra $200 a month to spend, I'd just end up buying things I don't need. When I know I'll have to give it to the mortgage company, then I won't waste it. Having the mortgage keeps me from wasting my money!"

As I said, we each know ourselves best, and we have to make our own decisions on the basis of what kind of people we are. We should keep in mind, however, that having the money on hand instead of in real estate puts us in a far better position in terms of liquidity. If there's a medical emergency or an investment opportunity, we have ready money to take care of the situation.

Assuming that you do decide to get a mortgage (and you may not) and put a smaller amount down, the next question that naturally arises is, "What should I do with my money?"

Most people usually just stick it in a bank or savings and loan association. In the next chapter we'll see why that can be the wrong thing to do.

ELEVEN

Inflation versus Retirement Dollars

Most people arrive at retirement with their pockets full of money. They may have a reduced income from pensions and social security, but in terms of cash, they're usually sitting on top of the world. They've sold their former home and they have up to $100,000 tax-free, some much more.

It always reminds me of the chipmunk. That lively animal spends the entire summer working hard to gather nuts and acorns for the long winter. It carefully stores them in hollows in trees. Finally, when the weather turns cold, the chipmunk stops working and looks at what it has accomplished—an enormous storehouse of food, enough to last it through the cold winter months.

Most of us are like chipmunks in this sense, we work hard all our lives and accumulate a certain amount of wealth, usually in our homes. When we sell our homes at retirement, it's like the chipmunk's storehouse. We look at the money we've received and gleam with pleasure at the thought that it will last us through retirement. That, however, is where the similarity ends.

If the chipmunk has gathered 100 nuts, assuming they don't spoil, he'll have 100 nuts available throughout the winter.

If, however, we've gathered $100,000, chances are within 10 years we'll only have $50,000, even if we never spend a penny of it. The reason, of course, is inflation.

The cruelest part of dwindling retirement dollars, in terms of cash reserves as well as pension income, is that most people do not see that it's happening. They, in fact, believe that the ravages of inflation are largely exaggerated or are happening to someone else's money. Inflation occurs so slowly that it is an almost invisible enemy. It's only after 5 or 10 years have passed and we go to buy something with our retirement funds that its effects are truly felt.

In this chapter, we're going to examine just how inflation affects retirement dollars. There will be no sleight of hand; the figures used will be accurate and real. I guarantee that if you have any doubts about how even moderate inflation touches you, they will be cleared up here.

LIFESTYLE AND INFLATION

I believe that the reason it's so hard to see inflation in the early days of retirement is because of our preretirement lifestyle. When we're working most of us become used to living off a salary. So much comes in each month and so much goes out. We scrimp to save a little, but mostly we budget. After 30 or 40 years, as I noted earlier, we become terrific budgeters. Given certain unchangeable facts—that we'll have an income each month, that the income will increase as our salary goes up—we become very capable at getting along, even improving our lives.

At retirement, however, the facts of life change. The salary is gone. It is replaced by a pension that in many cases either does not go up with the cost of living or goes up more slowly (this is not the pension plan's fault, as we'll see). In addition, for the first time in our lives, when we sell our house, we have a big bundle of cash to deal with. Spending 40 years living on a budget in no way prepares us to handle a large lump sum of money. The skills we've developed, in fact, may be harmful.

When we're working for a salary, most of us do not have large cash reserves. We may have a few thousand in the bank along the way, but rarely will any one of us have up to $100,000 or more. On those occasions when we find that we do have big reserves, we usually say to ourselves, "At last we're getting ahead." We tend to look at any big bundle of money as evidence that we're increasing our income, getting ahead of inflation, improving our lifestyle.

At retirement, our perceptions tend not to change. We see that big lump sum of money from the sale of our house and again we think we're getting ahead. Unfortunately, nothing could be further from the truth. A large lump sum of money in the bank *after retirement* usually means that you're falling behind, not getting ahead. It means that the money is gradually being diminished by inflation—that we're losing it.

For most people, having a lot of money in the bank seems like security. In reality, it's just the opposite. Most retirees are at their richest at the moment they retire. After that point they simply get poorer and poorer.

INFLATION AND SAVINGS ACCOUNTS

Let's look for a moment at savings accounts—in a bank, a savings and loan, a credit union, or wherever. There are essentially three reasons that people stick money into a savings account: security, availability, and interest. Security comes from the fact that we believe that no one can steal it, and in most cases, if the depository goes broke, the government will guarantee our funds. Availability is another word for liquidity that we examined in the last chapter. It simply means that we can get our cash when we want it, usually on a moment's notice (although most savings and loans associations and banks reserve the right to refuse to give us our money for up to 30 days should they be faced with a financial crisis and have trouble raising it).

Interest

Finally, there is interest. Interest is paid to us by the depository for the privilege of having our money. If we deposit $100,000 at 8 percent interest, at the end of one year we expect at least $108,000, much more if it's compounded. Where does the savings and loan association, for example, get that $8,000 or more it pays us?

Of course, as everyone knows, the savings and loan association makes real estate loans. It lends money out at, presumably, a higher rate of interest than it has to pay on deposits. Thereby it is able to pay our interest. We could, of course, make real estate loans ourselves and avoid the savings and loan. Many people do. But most people prefer to have the savings and loan association handle the loan process and that's why such associations are called "intermediaries." They are in between the person who has the capital (the retiree) and the person who borrows the money and pays interest on it. For their efforts, they take a certain portion of the interest that comes in from loans as their operating expenses and profits. Banks and credit unions operate essentially the same way.

Interest is as important as security and availability. It is the investment aspect or our capital. It's how we make our money grow.

The real question is, are we getting enough interest to justify our deposits?

To see what I mean, let's consider interest for a moment. What would you consider to be a good rate of *real* interest on your money? Would it be 8 percent? 10 percent? 15 or 18 percent?

If you felt that any of these figures were about right, then you need to reconsider what *real* interest is. Many economists and even many bankers would say that a good rate of *real* interest is between 1 and 2 percent! If you get that return, you're doing fairly well. Any more is just gravy.

At this point, if you're beginning to feel better about that 5 percent available from most banks in their regular passbook savings accounts, don't. The operative word in the last two paragraphs is *real*. What do I mean by *real* interest? Quite simply it is the rate of return after the money invested has been adjusted for any loss due to inflation.

Inflation

Inflation means the loss in value of our money. It isn't that chickens or dishwashers or autos are necessarily any more valuable today than they were last year. It's that the money we use to buy them with has lost some of its value. Therefore, it takes more money to buy the same items. Although we see this as an increase in price, it's actually a reduction in the value of money. There is, in fact, no way to measure inflation directly. We can only measure it indirectly as prices increases. That's why the most commonly used yardstick for inflation is the CPI, the consumer price index.

Real Interest

When we speak of real interest on money, we're talking about the return we would get if there were no inflation. For example, let's say we had $100,000 to invest and we wanted to get a 2 percent *real* return on that money. At the end of a year, if we had $102,000 we would have achieved our goal. But, only if there had been no inflation, only if the value of our money had not decreased, only if the consumer price index increase had been zero.

But, as we all know, the consumer price index hasn't been zero for nearly 40 years. In recent years the government has issued statements that inflation was under control when the consumer price index dipped below 10 percent. Therefore, as an arbitrary figure, let's assume that inflation is zipping along at 10 percent. We still want to earn 2 percent real interest. But, if at the end of a year our $100,000 has only turned to $102,000, we're far from our goal. In terms of value, if money had depreciated by 10 percent during the same time, what bought $100,000 a year ago only buys about $90,000 today. Our $102,000 in terms of buying power is really worth 10 percent or $10,200 less. Our $102,000 in cash is worth only about $92,000 in buying power. We haven't achieved our goal of getting a 2 percent *real* return at all. We've, in fact, lost about 8 percent of our capital.

Nominal Dollars

To put it more precisely, while our *nominal* dollars increased by two percent or $2,000, our *real* dollars decreased by $8,000. While our *nominal* rate of interest was 2 percent, our *real* rate of interest was minus 8 percent.

Nominal dollars	*Real dollars*
$100,000	$100,000
+ 2,000 interest	– 8,000 inflation
$102,000	$ 92,000

Nominal interest rate	*Real interest rate*
+ 2%	– 8%

What we must be concerned with is not nominal dollars (the actual number of dollars we have), but real dollars (their buying power). This is an easy concept to understand, but a hard concept to apply. When we see our nominal dollars jumping, for example, from $1,000 to $1,500 we're all apt to stand up and cheer. It looks as if we've increased our money by 50 percent. But, if at the same time inflation were to be moving at 50 percent, it would mean that our increase was actually zero. We had more dollars, but they were worth far less. It was nothing to cheer about after all.

Real versus Nominal

Let's return to our original question. How much money do we have to get to receive a *real* interest rate of 2 percent assuming inflation is at 10 percent?

The answer is approximately 12 percent (I say approximately because we're making all calculations on an annual basis and there would be compounding of monies during the year). In order to return a 2 percent *real* rate of interest, we'd have to get a 12 percent *nominal* rate of interest.

Nominal interest rate	12%
Lost to inflation	10%
Real interest rate	2%

Nominal dollars	*Real dollars*
$100,000	$100,000
+ 12,000 (12% interest)	+ 2,000 (2% interest)
$112,000	$102,000

Note that in the above figures, the number of dollars we would have (nominal) would jump by $12,000. But, the real dollars or the value of the money in terms of buying power, would only go up by about $2,000.

Put most simply, in order to get a real interest rate of 2 percent, we have to be earning 2 percent more than the rate of inflation, whatever it might be. Anything less and we don't get our return. Even more important, *if we earn anything less than the rate of inflation, we are actually losing real dollars.*

Now, let's apply this to savings accounts. The computations are extremely easy. If a savings account is yielding 5 percent (nominal interest) and inflation is at a 10 percent rate, what is the *real* interest rate?

Savings account yield	5%
Less inflation rate	10%
Real interest	− 5%

In real life most passbook savings accounts do, in fact, only yield about 5 percent, and inflation in the last few years has been running 10 percent or higher. People who have had their money deposited in such an account have been losing about 5 percent.

But, it could be argued, that's not really fair. Most savings and loan associations as well as banks offer much higher interest rates on long-term accounts. In fact, many such institutions offer "T-bill" accounts for money deposited for as short a time as six months.

Treasury Bills

A T-bill account is simply a deposit on which the interest paid is tied to the interest rate on six-month Treasury bills during the week the money was deposited. Treasury bills are basically short-term government bonds. They are borrowings by the federal government. They are usually issued in three- or six-month periods and are available to absolutely anyone who can come up with the $10,000 minimum (larger T-bills are available in increments of $5,000). Often the highest nonrisk interest rate (deposit or bank time accounts) is paid on T-bills and T-bill accounts.

I've watched T-bills closely over the last few years and I've found that the T-bill rate always seems to be below the rate of inflation. In fact I've charted the T-bill rate and the inflation rate, and the results are rather interesting.

INFLATION RATE VERSUS T-BILL INTEREST RATE*

Although T-bill rates occasionally come close to matching inflation, they never seem to quite do it. In fact, in most cases they are 2 or more percentage points below the rate of inflation. All of which is to say that even if we put money in the highest-yield T-bill deposits in savings and loan associations and banks, we are still losing to inflation, losing much more than most of us realize. (See Table 11-1.)

---

*Sources: The T-bill rate is from U.S. Financial Data, Federal Reserve Bank of Detroit, July 9, 1980. The inflation rate is the consumer price index listed in Economic Indicators, U.S. Government Printing Office, June, 1980.

MEASURING THE LOSS TO INFLATION OF MONEY IN A SAVINGS ACCOUNT

How much is the loss? The greatest differential during the period I charted between T-bills and inflation was about 5 percent. On the average the difference was closer to about 3 percent. That doesn't seem like such a great amount to lose, 3 percent a year. Or does it? Just how much is a three percent a year loss to inflation over a 10-year period?

Table 11-1 shows $100,000 and the amount it would lose over 10 years if the rate of inflation were only 3 percent (compounded annually).

A 3 percent inflation rate compounded annually (the loss would be higher if compounded daily as is done in real life) would mean that at the end of 10 years, we would have lost nearly a fourth of our money!

It must be kept in mind that Table 11-1 shows only *real* dollars. It assumes that we did not deposit our money nor receive any interest on it and that the inflation rate was only 3 percent. Another way (Table 11-2) to look at the same information is to assume that we deposited our money in an account that pays 3 percent less than the going rate of

TABLE 11-1 DEPRECIATION OF $100,000 AT 3% ANNUALLY

Year	Amount
1	$100,000
2	97,000
3	94,090
4	91,267
5	88,429
6	85,873
7	83,297
8	80,798
9	78,374
10	76,023

TABLE 11-2

Year	Savings account at 9% nominal dollars in acount	Inflation rate at 12% real dollars in account in terms of original buying power
1	$100,000	$100,000
2	109,000	97,000
3	118,810	94,090
4	129,503	91,267
5	141,158	88,429
6	153,862	85,873
7	167,710	83,297
8	182,804	80,879
9	199,256	78,374
10	217,189	76,023

inflation. Let's assume we deposit our $100,000 at 9 percent interest and the rate of inflation is 12 percent. We'll further assume both inflation and interest are compounded annually and that the rates do not change for a 10-year period.

In this far more dramatic example we see that although the money in our savings account has more than doubled in the 10-year period in terms of *nominal* dollars, it has shrunk to only 75 percent of its former self in terms of *real* dollars. Another way of saying this is that in terms of this chart, what will cost $217,000 10 years from today, only costs about $76,000 today. There is a $24,000 loss in *real* money at the same time there is a $117,000 increase in *nominal* dollars. Inflation has taken away more than the interest rate has put into our account.

Finally, in Table 11-3 we'll look at the same information in terms of what items will cost along the way. We'll assume that the base year is now and that inflation moves along at an annual rate of 12 percent. What will $100,000 in real money buy tomorrow?

We would need $277,000 to equal the buying power of $100,000 after 10 years, assuming 12 percent inflation. As we've already seen,

TABLE 11-3

Year	What it costs in nominal dollars to buy the same amount of goods as in year 1 (12% inflation)	Money from savings deposited at 9% (see Table 11-2)
1	$100,000	$100,000
2	112,000	109,000
3	125,440	118,810
4	140,493	129,503
5	157,351	141,158
6	176,234	153,862
7	197,382	167,710
8	221,068	182,804
9	247,596	199,256
10	277,307	217,189

by depositing our money at 9 percent interest, after 10 years we only have $217,000—far short.

What should be obvious from these charts is that we eventually go broke if we deposit our money in a savings account that pays even just a few percentage points of interest lower than the rate of inflation. Remember, in these charts the differential between the interest we received on our savings account and the rate of inflation was only 3 percent.

It should also be obvious that we should not be fooled by nominal amounts of money. At 9 percent interest after 10 years it may seem that the $217,000 we'll get back is a wondrous sum of money. But, that's only because we're thinking in terms of the $100,000 we started with in year 1. If we compare it to what's really required in terms of buying power, we see that in order to have the same $100,000 in year 10, we would need $277,307 dollars—a far cry from what we actually have.

What would happen to the real buying power of $100,000 if the differential between inflation and interest received were other than 3 percent? Table 11-4 assumes that we've deposited our money in a 5 percent passbook account. It gives the real value of that money at different inflation rates. To find the differential, simply subtract the rate of inflation from the interest being paid. At 7 percent inflation the differential is 2 percent; at 15 percent inflation the differential is 10 percent. (Please note that the figures given under *real* value of $100,000 take into account the *increase* in dollars put into the savings account each year. If we didn't take this into account the money would dwindle to nothing in far less than 10 years!)

(Each year the nominal dollars in the savings account increase. Yet, the real buying power of those dollars goes down in terms of the year when the money was first deposited.)

If there is anything I would like you to come away with from all these charts and figures, it is the knowledge that keeping money in a

TABLE 11-4 REAL VALUE OF $100,000 ASSUMING ANNUAL INFLATION RATES OF VARYING AMOUNTS COMPOUNDED ANNUALLY IN TERMS OF BUYING POWER

Year	*Savings account 5% (compounded annually):* nominal amounts	*Real value at various inflation rates*			
		7%	*10%*	*15%*	*18%*
0	$100,000	$100,000	$100,000	$100,000	$100,000
1	105,000	97,650	95,000	89,250	86,100
2	110,250	95,366	89,303	79,601	74,088
3	115,763	93,735	84,391	71,078	63,785
4	121,551	91,078	79,877	63,560	55,037
5	127,624	88,702	75,301	56,667	47,350
6	134,010	86,704	71,154	50,522	40,739
7	140,711	84,567	67,260	45,028	35,037
8	147,747	82,591	63,531	40,187	30,140
9	155,133	80,664	60,036	35,991	26,062
10	162,890	78,839	56,849	32,084	22,316

savings account where the interest is lower than the rate of inflation *always* means you lose.

That does not mean you shouldn't put your money in a savings account. You'll recall that there were at least two other reasons for depositing money in such an account besides collecting interest—availability and security. The money will be there when you want to take it out. It's just that in terms of real dollars, there will be less and less to take out. That is why finding investment strategies to beat inflation is so important.

INCOME

Unfortunately, the same attack that inflation makes on our savings accounts, it also makes on our income, whether from social security, pensions, or whatever. Of course, people on a fixed income don't have to be told this. They see it in the form of increased food costs, higher medical bills, higher gas and transportation prices, and on and on. For a person just considering retirement, however, it may not be so obvious. For that reason, let's consider inflation and retirement income. To begin, we'll assume that our retirement income is fixed, that it doesn't go up in any significant amount.

Special note! This is not to criticize retirement plans. As we'll see, inflation makes it virtually impossible for all but the exceptional plan to keep up. It's simply to show that after you retire it is unrealistic to believe that your pension plan will be able to keep up with inflation.

Once again, we're going to use the terms real and nominal. Real will mean the actual buying power of our income. Nominal will mean the actual dollars that we receive. For example, let's say we receive $100 per month. That's the money we get in terms of *nominal* dollars. But inflation is running at 10 percent, so our dollars are worth 10 percent less at the end of the year. They're only worth $90. That's our *real* income.

$100	nominal dollars
−10%	inflation rate
$ 90	real dollars

The effects of this can be clearly seen if we take an individual whose fixed income is $1,000 a year. This person receives that much money each year. Now, in Table 11-5 we'll compare this $1,000 to the amount the person actually gets in terms of buying power at various rates of inflation.

What should be immediately obvious is that even at a relatively modest inflation rate of 7 percent, the *real* income has been cut in half after the end of 10 years by inflation. Although we still receive $1,000 in cash, it buys only $484 worth of goods and services when compared to 10 years earlier. At an inflation rate of 13 percent, buying power is cut from $1,000 to $248 over 10 years, and so on. At an average inflation rate of 7 percent annually, in order to buy the same amount, the individual's pension would have had to double to more than $2,000 a month over the 10 years! At the annual rate of inflation of 13 percent, we would have to quadruple our income to $4,000 a year to equal the same buying power as $1,000 did before.

The real power of this chart, however, shows up in the lower rates of inflation. It shows just how much even a relatively small rate of inflation can eat away at retirement income.

TABLE 11-5 REAL INCOME AT DIFFERENT RATES OF INFLATION

Year	Nominal income	7%	10%	13%	18%	20%
1	$1,000	$930	$900	$870	$820	$800
2	1,000	865	810	757	672	640
3	1,000	804	729	659	551	512
4	1,000	748	656	573	452	410
5	1,000	695	590	498	371	328
6	1,000	647	531	434	304	262
7	1,000	601	478	377	249	210
8	1,000	554	430	328	204	168
9	1,000	520	387	286	168	134
10	1,000	484	349	248	137	107

INDEXING

Fortunately, many retirement plans, including social security, are indexed. That means that they increase in income according to the depreciation in the value of the dollar. If inflation runs at a rate of, for example, 12 percent, income is increased by 12 percent. It is only by such indexing that people on pensions can hope to keep their income even with inflation. (Investing is another alternative, as we'll see in the next two chapters.) Maintaining this increase, however, is driving social security to bankruptcy.

Some retirement income, however, is not indexed to the rate of inflation, but rather to an arbitrary figure. It just goes up a certain amount, such as 5 percent or 7 percent, each year. This can be fine as long as inflation is at or lower than the arbitrary figure. However, when inflation goes higher, it can have a devastating effect on retirement income. Table 11-6 shows a retirement income that increases automatically by 5 percent annually and the results when compared to various rates of inflation.

TABLE 11-6   REAL INCOME REQUIRED TO EQUAL $1,000 OF BUYING POWER AT DIFFERENT ANNUAL INFLATION RATES

Year	Nominal monthly income (increased by 5% annually)	Real income at different inflation rates			
		7%	*10%*	*13%*	*18%*
1	$1,000	$1070	$1100	$1130	$1180
2	1,050	1145	1210	1277	1180
3	1,103	1225	1331	1443	1643
4	1,158	1311	1464	1630	1939
5	1,216	1403	1611	1842	2288
6	1,276	1501	1772	2082	2700
7	1,340	1606	1949	2353	3185
8	1,407	1718	2144	2658	3759
9	1,477	1838	2358	3004	4435
10	1,551	1967	2594	3395	5234

Even if the differential between inflation and the retirement income is only 2 percent (income increases by 5 percent annually, inflation by 7 percent) at the end of 10 years it will take $1,967 to buy what it originally took $1,000 to buy—but the income will only be $1,551. There will be a loss in nominal dollars of over $400 in order to keep even in real buying power. If inflation were to run at 18 percent annually, the loss would be far greater. It would take $5,234 to buy in 10 years what it takes $1,000 to buy today. At an income (at 5 percent increases per year) of $1,551, the difference is a shortage of $3,683 nominal dollars per year. Of course, once again, the power of this chart is not in the area of great differentials, but of small ones. It can be a real eye-opener to see how even a differential of only 2 percent can mean a big difference over a period of 10 years.

As I noted, much retirement income is indexed in one form or another. The problem is that it is difficult for retirement plans to pay increasing amounts each year. Remember, each year more and more people come onto such plans. To pay more and more people increasing amounts of money is simply an impossibility in most cases. That's one of the reasons that social security is in such a bad way today. It simply bankrupts the retirement plan to fully index all pensioners. In most cases those managing the program simply can't invest the money quickly enough to make ends meet. That's why it is unrealistic for those facing retirement to expect their retirement income to keep up with inflation.

It's normally not the fault of the retirement program or its administrators. It's simply in the nature of inflation itself. In order to keep retirement income up, retirees themselves must consider prudent investments.

Many individuals and families are already involved in a variety of retirement programs. These include annuities, investments in stocks and bonds, and real estate, as well as exotic investments such as coins, stamps, gold, and silver. If you currently don't have a financial plan for retirement, my suggestion is that you immediately consult with your financial adviser (attorney, accountant, or whomever you use). For those interested in investing in real estate I also suggest my recent book, *Riches in Real Estate: A Beginner's Guide to Group Investing* (McGraw-Hill, 1980).

TWELVE

Making Your Housing Decision

The decision to sell a home and try a particular housing alternative for retirement is based on different factors for each of us. In the first part of this book we saw how a couple, Marge and Peter, discovered what the up to $100,000 exclusion was and how to use it. Then we went on to watch as they considered different types of retirement houses. Eventually, they opted for a condominium. (See Chapter 9.)

While some of the considerations that led them to select a condo may be similar to your own, others may be totally different. A condominium may, in fact, not be your retirement home choice. The factors that influence your decision are unique. While Marge and Peter can well serve as an example to help you discover what alternatives are available, they make rather poor models when it comes to helping you reach your own personal decision.

To help you find out what type of housing you are most likely to desire and need, this chapter presents a series of self-evaluation checklists. We'll consider your actual housing requirements, your psychological support system, your community needs, your social requirements, and finally your financial condition.

These checklists are presented with open spaces for you to write in your answers. Since these answers are unique to you, the composite sketch they will eventually create should help make it easier for you to determine what your $100,000 decision should be. It is suggested that after completing the questions and after you have a good idea of what your desires and needs really are, you return to the lists at the end of the chapters on housing. This will help you to find the most appropriate alternative.

One note about filling out these checklists. Honesty is absolutely necessary. This is not a test, nor are there any right or wrong answers. No one comes out winning or losing. Rather, it is simply an opportunity to discover where you are in terms of retirement housing.

I know that I myself have a tendency to answer personal questions in such a way that they portray me as I wish I were, rather than as I really am—but these questions, if answered honestly, may produce some surprises. You may discover that what you really want and need in housing is considerably different from what you thought.

Finally, please keep in mind that since this is a self-test, the only person who need see the answers is you. Anything that you hide, you are only hiding from yourself.

Caution: These questions are simply designed as quick aids to indicate directions you might want to pursue further in housing. They should not be applied to any other area, should not be considered conclusive, nor should they be relied upon as the primary determiner of your housing needs.

HOUSING REQUIREMENTS CHECKLIST

What shape and form should the house you buy take? In the early chapters, Marge and Peter examined housing alternatives with an eye toward finding the right size, features, number of stories, and so forth, for them. But, what do you personally want out of the physical structure of your retirement home?

To help uncover your real needs and wants, I've put together this "housing requirements checklist." Having sold real estate and having spent many years working with brokers and buyers, I find these questions to be very helpful in determining the physical requirements of the house:

Mobility

1. Do you find it difficult walking up stairs? Yes____, No____.

2. Will you or any member of your family who will live with you be required to use any apparatus to aid walking, such as a wheelchair or walker? Yes____, No____.

3. Do you have any leg, back, or other ailments that limit mobility? Yes___, No___.

4. What will your age be upon retirement? ___

These first four questions are designed to help determine whether you should get a single-level home, or one with two or more stories. If you answered yes to any question, you will probably want a single-level home. Additionally, if you answered "over 65" to the age question you may want to seriously consider a single-level home regardless of your present mobility. It simply is a fact of life that as we get older, we tend to acquire injuries and illnesses that restrict our mobility. Even though you may be in perfect health today, it's wise to keep an eye on the future. Just falling and twisting an ankle while playing tennis or even golf could make a two-story home a nightmare.

There are a few other important considerations if mobility is a problem. One of them is the type of floor the new home will have. Highly polished hardwood, tile, or linoleum floors can be slippery, particularly if something spills on them. A wet floor, of course, is a hazard at any age and condition of health, but for someone who has trouble getting around it can be a death trap.

Floors that are carpeted tend to be less slippery, although heavy carpeting such as shag produces the new problem of tripping. Some feel that a compromise that works is a tight, short carpet.

Additionally, there is a matter of the availability of handrails in the bathroom. Some bathrooms are tiny and are really too small to accommodate handrails (or grips). While this may not be a problem upon purchase, if these devices become necessary at a later date, the home can become instantly obsolete. Buying a home with a big enough bathroom now can save expensive problems later on.

Finally, there is the matter of the kitchen. Counterspace and shelves that are of an appropriate height to avoid much leaning or bending can be very beneficial if there is a mobility problem.

Noise

5. Do you let your television or radio play loudly for several hours a day? Yes___, No___.

6. Do others who let their radios or TVs blare loudly bother you? Yes___, No___.

7. When grandchildren or children of friends come over to visit you, does the noise of their play bother you? (Be truthful. It's not a matter of whether or not you love children. It's simply a matter of noise.) Yes___, No___.

8. Is your hearing excellent? Yes___, No___.

The purpose of these four questions is to help determine whether your retirement home should have strict sound control. Many of you will answer no to most of the above questions. You really don't care much about sound one way or the other. But some people are very sensitive to sound. (I'm one of those. I don't mind making a lot of noise myself, but I don't want to hear anyone else's noise.)

If you've answered yes to most of the above questions, you will probably want to seriously consider a single-family home. If you are leaning toward a mobile home, a condominium, or an apartment, you will want to pay special attention to the noise potential. Are children allowed? If they are, noise could be a big problem. Have you walked through the area listening? Do neighbors have their TVs or radios on loud? Do you hear arguments and boisterous talks through open windows?

Good sound insulation is very expensive and seldom built into any kind of home units. In most cases sound control has to be obtained by eliminating the noise source. In many cases with high density (see Chapter 5) this is impossible.

If you move into a unit that has poor noise control, your retirement years could be very upsetting.

Light

9. When you read, do you find that you like to sit by a window? Yes___, No___ .

10. Do you like being able to walk over to a window and look out? (Do you leave your curtains open a great deal, as opposed to keeping them shut most of the time?) Yes___, No___.

11. Do you like the room you live in to be light and airy? (Do you avoid rooms in which the light is calmer and more subdued)? Yes___, No___.

We're trying to determine whether you should pay special attention to the amount of window space available in your new home. Today, for conservation reasons, many newer homes are built with much less window space than in the past. Some people don't mind this and like the savings it offers in heating and cooling costs, but others need the light that comes from large windows. It's a serious consideration in retirement homes since the amount of light coming in from outside can have a big affect on your mood.

Size

12. Do you really require more than one bedroom for your family needs? Yes____, No____ .

13. Do you serve formal meals in a dining room at least once a month? Yes____, No____ .

14. Do you sit in and use a formal living room more than once a month? Yes____, No____ .

15. Do you use more than one bathroom in your present home on a regular basis? Yes____, No____ .

16. Do you have company that stays overnight more than once every few months? Yes____, No____ .

Features

17. Do you use your fireplace more than once a month? Yes____, No____ .

18. Do you park your car in your garage regularly? Yes____, No____ .

19. Is your garage used primarily as a storage area, and if you move, will you need to take most of the material stored there with you? Yes____, No____ .

20. Do you regularly make big meals in your kitchen using large amounts of counter space? Yes____, No____ .

The purpose of these nine questions is to discover just what your housing needs really are (as opposed to what you're currently used to). If you answered yes to most questions, chances are you're going to need a large home. On the other hand, if most of your answers are no, you probably will be able to get by with a minimal amount of living space. Your options are quite open since most housing alternatives come in all sizes. However, since price is directly related to size, if you can get by with less size, you can save a great deal of money.

Questions 12 through 16 relate to the number of bedrooms and other rooms in your home. If you only use one bedroom and you infrequently have guests (who could sleep on a rollaway in the living room when they do come), why pay more for a home that has more than one or two bedrooms?

Similarly, if you don't use a formal dining room or living room, why pay more for a home that offers these features?

Questions 17 through 20 relate to other features that add to cost, such as a fireplace, an enclosed garage, and a large kitchen. If you don't use these features, why pay for them in a retirement home?

A point here might be raised by some readers who would argue that it's important to "overbuy" in a home in order to have a marketable house when it comes time to sell. In other words, it's important to buy a larger home to be able to find buyers later on. A small home can be a poor investment.

While this is certainly true for most home purchases, it is not true for a retirement home purchase. In a retirement home, buyers tend to be looking for small, not large.

Additionally, although you will probably get less for a minimum-size home when it comes times to sell, this is usually offset by the fact that you pay less when you buy.

Finally, in retirement homes, as in almost any other kind, factors such as location and the quality of surrounding units are often as important as, if not more important than, the size of the unit you are selling.

Climate

20. Do you mind very hot or cold weather? Yes___, No___.

21. Do you tend to spend a great deal of time indoors? Yes___, No___.

22. Are you sensitive to pollens, or do you have other airborne allergy problems? Yes___, No___.

These questions relate to the type of climate you may prefer and the degree of control over it you may want. Many people, particularly those from the Northern states, tend to dream of Southern warm climates to retire to. Their ideal may be Florida or Arizona or California.

However, the real question is not so much whether you want to go from cold to hot as whether you want to live in an area of temperature extremes. While the Northern states may have cold winters, many of the Southern states tend to have very hot summers and, particularly around the Gulf and the East Coast, very high humidity. For those sensitive to either heat or humidity, the Southern states can be just as undersirable as the cold of the Northern ones. A central state which can offer more moderate year-round temperatures is the preferred alternative for many people.

If you tend to live indoors a lot, of course, you have the opportunity of controlling your climate, and you will want to pay special attention to this in your retirement home. Today, air conditioning is a regular feature in many homes. It can reduce summer heat and humidity as well as allergens in the air (through filters). In colder climates a good heating system is something to pay particular attention to.

With both air conditioning and heating, attention should be paid to the "efficiency" of the unit. This simply means how much energy is required to produce a given amount of heating or cooling. With the costs of all energy shooting upward, a highly efficient unit can mean real savings. [Note: Efficiency does not simply mean using one type of energy source over another. In one part of the country natural gas may be the least expensive source, while in another, electricity may be cheaper, but what I'm speaking of here is how efficiently a unit uses energy regardless of the source. For example, two natural gas furnaces may produce the same number of BTUs (heat), but one may require a third more gas to do it. Naturally the more efficient unit would be more desirable. Many manufacturers today are rating the efficiency of their products.]

Safety

23. Are you concerned about your personal safety inside your own home? Yes___, No___.

Most people living in major cities in America today take the precaution of bolting doors and securing windows in their homes. However, some of us are more concerned about safety than others, and this concern tends to become more intense the older we get. Eventually, for some it reaches a point where heavy padlocks are not enough. We want the security that comes from knowing that there's somebody else nearby to call if an emergency occurs.

It should be noted that this fear of criminals by older Americans is not unwarranted. Crime statistics show that with age comes greater vulnerability to crime, particularly theft. Older people, whether married or single, can be prime targets for criminals.

If you're concerned about your personal safety in your home, then this concern can and should influence your housing decision. Many planned retirement communities offer 24-hour guard service. Gates control the entrance to the community, and patrol cars are on duty. Some condominiums and co-ops offer similar services, with guards at the doors and electronic surveillance and gates at the parking areas. In addition, some of these units offer alarm systems, as well as warning buttons in each unit that can be pushed to sound the alarm at a security guard's station.

Of course, if this seems like too much security (remember, you'll have to pay for what you get) there are compromises. Sometimes just living in an apartment or condo and knowing that there are other people all around is enough to make people feel secure. Or knowing that a manager is just a phone call away can be the thing that helps them to sleep well at night.

On the other hand, there are those who simply have no problems with security at all. Typically these people have been strong physically and emotionally all their lives and aren't changing now. In this case any type of housing, including single-family detached, is suitable.

Many factors influence the *physical* demands we make on a house. We've looked at mobility, concern about noise and light, need for size and other features (such as fireplaces), as well as desire for climate control and personal safety. While the ideal retirement choice (in terms of the physical home) would be a place that satisfied all needs and concerns, in most cases the actual home chosen ends up being a compromise. That means that you have to decide which of the areas you've covered are most important to you. You should put them in terms of your own personal priorities and then take a list of your priorities with you as a guide when you go shopping for your retirement home.

Choose the correct order for you from these concerns and needs:
Mobility
Noise
Light
Size
Features
Climate
Safety

PRIORITIES

1. _____

2. _____

3. _____

4. _____

5. _____

6. _____

7. _____

SUPPORT SYSTEM CHECKLIST

Let's now turn to the question of how far you are going to move away from your present home. This has to be a big consideration in choosing a retirement home. Chances are that, where you are now living, you have established an elaborate psychological support system (even if you're unaware of its existence). If so, moving away might be a traumatic experience, one that some of you may want to avoid.

The following questions are aimed at helping you discover the extent of your support system and giving you the opportunity to look at it and decide whether you really can bear to leave all or part of it behind.

List the names of relatives whom you regularly see (once a week or more), either by having them come to your house or by your going to theirs:

1. _____
2. _____
3. _____
4. _____
5. _____
6. _____
7. _____
8. _____
9. _____
10. _____

Now list the names of neighbors whom you contact either by going to their home, by having them visit yours, or by talking to them on the phone at least once a week. (Neighbors are usually those within walking distance of your home.):

1. _____
2. _____
3. _____
4. _____
5. _____
6. _____
7. _____
8. _____
9. _____
10. _____

Now list the names of friends with whom you have personal contact at least once every month, who live more than walking distance from you. (Examples of personal contact are a phone call, a dinner party, or just an evening spent talking with one another.):

1. _____
2. _____
3. _____

4. _____

5. _____

6. _____

7. _____

8. _____

9. _____

10. _____

Finally, list the names of any other people who come to see you or whom you visit on a regular basis and whom you consider closer than just a passing acquaintance. Don't include people such as mail deliverers, grocery clerks, insurance sales people, etc., unless they happen to be personal friends of yours:

1. _____

2. _____

3. _____

4. _____

5. _____

6. _____

7. _____

8. _____

9. _____

10. _____

The names you have listed above help form your psychological support base. These are the people who by their visits and the words they say give you support. Of course, this support may not always be obvious. Sometimes it simply takes the form of a conversation about the weather or a comment about world events. It may even be an unspeaking contact with another human being. What's important here is that each contact of whatever quality gives you an opportunity to not feel alone in the world. (Loneliness is listed by many retirees as their number one problem.) Also, the more contacts you have, the more opportunity you will have to present any concerns you have about medical problems, housing, food, or whatever to other people and get their reaction. Watching how others react to our concerns let's us know whether we're acting reasonably. It keeps us from losing ourselves in our own fears and worries.

If you plan to move any sizable distance from your present home (more than 25 miles away), the chances are that you will lose a substantial portion of the support base you've established. Most of the people you've placed on your list's will stop seeing you simply because it will be too difficult and inconvenient to come to where you are. At first, of course, there may be visits. But in the end, few will go as much as 25 miles to visit regularly, particularly friends.

If you move as much as 100 miles or more away, the chances are you won't see any of these people except on very rare occasions.

If you have filled up these pages with names of people you cherish, you ought to seriously consider the following questions: Will I be able to enjoy each and every day without these contacts? Will not seeing these people make me lonely? Permanently? Will I be able to make new friends to replace them?

If these questions bother you and you worry about losing your close contacts, you may want to reconsider staying close to where you are.

On the other hand, perhaps you have few or no names on these lists. Or, perhaps you've listed people, both relatives and friends, whom you'd rather not ever see again. (Just because someone comes to visit you, that doesn't mean you're happy to see them. Some relatives and so-called friends are really just pests whom you might prefer to do without.) In this case, maybe a move of considerable distance would be advised.

COMMUNITY SERVICES CHECKLIST

We've already considered the "support system" from the psychological viewpoint: how much of a strain it will be if you move away from friends and relatives. But there is another type of support that we all require: "community services." This is also an important factor in determining your ultimate housing requirements.

Most communities offer some forms of professional and recreational services, but not all offer all services. This checklist will help you determine some of the important services you use and will want to check out in considering any new home location.

Professional Services

1. Do you have a family physician whom you've known and relied upon for a long period of time? Yes___, No___.

2. Do you have any chronic ailment that requires special medical treatment? Yes___, No___.

3. Do you have a family dentist? Yes___, No___.

4. Have you known and dealt with your attorney over many years? Yes___, No___.

5. Do you have a real estate broker you rely on? Yes___, No___.

6. Have you dealt with your accountant over many years? Yes___, No___.

7. Do you regularly seek advice from a particular person in a bank, stock brokerage firm, or other financial institution? Yes___, No___.

If you answered "no" to most of these questions, then a move to a new community away from where you are living probably won't be made more difficult by the loss of service of particular professionals.

On the other hand, if your answers tended to be yes, then you may want to carefully consider any long-distance move. It's not always easy to establish good new relationships with professionals.

Trying to hang onto old relationships may not work well either. Commuting great distances to see a favorite doctor, dentist, or attorney usually doesn't work out.

Recreational Services

8. Is there a community center nearby that you visit at least twice a month? Yes___, No___.

9. Are there organized sports, lectures, special plays or movies, or other recreational activities in which you regularly participate where you now live? Yes___, No___.

10. Is there a track nearby at which you regularly jog, or are there tennis courts where you play or a park where you walk, etc.? Yes___, No___.

These questions relate to community services that you may regularly enjoy, but seldom think about. It is important to consider them when thinking of moving. If you answered yes to most of the questions, will a new area you're moving to offer similar services? If not, can you comfortably do without them?

Again, these considerations are not likely to keep you from moving a great distance away. But, when measured with other concerns, they can be a strong influence.

SOCIABILITY CHECKLIST

The type of housing you ultimately choose may have a big influence on your lifestyle. Single-family homes on occasion can isolate a person. On the other hand, condominiums or mobile homes sometimes can offer enormous social opportunities. Depending on your personality, these different types of housing can be appealing or unappealing. To help determine which type of housing you may be leaning toward, I've come up with what I call a sociability checklist.

There are many commercial tests available to help us determine just how gregarious we really are. Although this one is certainly far from foolproof, I like it because, unlike any other I've seen, it's specifically keyed to housing.

Check the box A, B, or C, as appropriate:

1. How many times a week do you go over to a neighbor's home to chat? Less than once___A, two to three times___B, four or more times___C.

2. How many times a week does a neighbor come to visit you for just a chat? Less than once___A, two to three times___B, four or more times___C.

3. How many times a week do you play bridge, poker, rummy, or other social card game? Less than once___A, two to three times___B, four or more times___C.

4. How many times a month do you attend parties (including a gathering of friends, church or synagogue activities, formal weddings, etc.)? Less than once___A, two to three times___B, four or more times___C.

5. How many social organizations or clubs do you belong to and regularly attend meetings? Less than once___A, two to three times___B, four or more times___C.

6. How many hours a day do you spend at home watching television? Four or more___A, two to three___B, one or less___C.

7. How many hours a day do you spend at home reading, sewing or other-

wise by yourself? Four or more____A, two to three____B, one or less____C.

8. If there are neighborhood barbecues, picnics, community meetings, dances, etc., available to you, how many of the last five invitations have you accepted? One or less____A, two to three____B, four to five____C.

9. In the last year, how many meetings of your city council, boy scout organization, park and recreational council, charity association, or other group involving a commitment of time and effort in organizing have you attended? One or less____A, two to three____B, four or more____C.

10. How would you rate your personality? Keep to myself____A, average____B, outgoing____C.

To rate this test simply add up all the check marks in boxes A, then all the checks in B, then all the checks in C. If you have a preponderance in A, I would guess that you would probably prefer a lifestyle that involves isolated housing such as a single-family detached home or a planned unit development (townhouse). You might find the communal aspects of condos, co-ops, retirement communities, and even mobile home parks a bit trying and uncomfortable.

On the other hand, if most of your answers were in the C boxes, then I'd guess that you'd tend to be just the opposite. You'd probably prefer the gregarious lifestyle opportunities that many condos and similar alternatives offer. You might find the single-family detached home too isolated.

If most of your answers were B, you probably could go either way.

A note of caution: This short test should not be considered conclusive in any sense, and you shouldn't rely on it. The best advice I can give is that if you feel inclined toward any particular kind of housing alternative, take it for a trial period. Almost anywhere you can find units to rent. Rent one for a few months. You'll quickly find out whether or not it's for you.

FINANCIAL CHECKLIST

For most of us, money is the most important concern. Of course, I think we realize that money can't solve all our problems; but it is a fact that having enough money can make retirement much easier, and it certainly can give us more options in our choice of housing.

This checklist gives you the opportunity to try to determine just how much money you can reasonably expect to have available for retirement. Then we'll consider how this affects your housing choice.

Monthly Income and Cash Reserves

1. Name the pensions (or other sources) that you will have available to provide you with income during retirement—give the *exact* amount of money you can expect to receive from each (as of this date):

A. Social Security $_____

B. _____   _____

C. _____   _____

D. _____   _____

E. _____   _____

Total $_____

If you're 55, or nearing the age of retirement, one important thing you should know is how much money you can expect each month after you retire. Of course, the actual money may change by the time you finally do retire. But, in order to make a sound plan, you should at least know what you'll be getting as of this date.

I emphasized the word "exact" in the earlier paragraph not because I think knowing the amount down to the penny will make any great difference in your choices, but because of the tendency that many of us have to "guestimate." Someone recently said to me, "Well, I'll be getting around $300 from social security and about another $700 from my pension." Upon finding out the exact figures, this person discovered that social security would be paying $389 and the pension plan would provide $811. The guestimator was a total of $200 a month off, because the guess was $1,000 a month, and the actual figure was $1,200 a month—a substantial error that could make a big difference when determining housing alternatives.

Once you know what income you will have, recheck Chapter 10 to see how big a mortgage you can safely qualify for.

2. How much cash do you have in the bank, mutual funds, etc.?

$ _____

3. What is the cash value of any insurance policies that you have?

$_____

4. What is the value of any stocks, bonds, trust deeds, rare coins, stamps, or other securities you may own?

$ _____

Total $ _____

These figures should give you a good idea of your liquid asset position. "Liquid assets" simply means cash or money that you can immediately (or in a very short while) put your hands on. This is money that you can keep in reserve after you purchase a retirement home, or money that you may want to use as part of your down payment.

Nonliquid Reserves

5. After the one-in-a-lifetime up to $100,000 exclusion, what is the after-sales-expenses* value of the equity† in your home? (See Chapter 1 for a definition of equity.)

$ _____

---

*The sales expenses involved in selling a home and most other types of real estate are often between 7 and 10 percent, with about 8 percent being average. This includes real estate sales commission, escrow and title fees, recording fees, termite clearance, and other closing costs.

†The best way to find the actual equity of your home is to hire a professional appraiser, usually one who has an MAI or SRA designation. Or you can save the few hundred dollars this may cost and figure it out for yourself. Just locate other homes that are very similar to your own that have sold recently and compare prices. Of course, this can be tricky since very few homes are identical and locations are unique. A guide to this self-appraisal can be found in Robert Irwin's *How to Buy a Home at a Reasonable Price*, McGraw-Hill, 1979. Many real estate agents will also give free appraisals; however, my experience has been that these are too often clouded by the agent's desire to get a listing.

6. What is the after-tax, ‡ after-sales-expenses (see footnote* on page 179) value of your equity in other real estate?

$ _____

Total $ _____

Questions 5 and 6 represent your nonliquid assets or the money you have which may take some time to convert into cash. (Selling your real estate could take many months). Once turned into cash, this money can be used just by itself to purchase a new retirement home (see Chapter 2 for rolling over principal residences) or it can be used in conjunction with your liquid assets. Or only a portion of this money might be used to make a purchase of a home, the remainder converted to liquid reserves to be used for investment.

Once you know how much your liquid and nonliquid assets are, you are in a position to consider how big a down payment to go for. Recheck Chapter 10 for other considerations, but keep in mind that you will not want to plunk all your money down into a home if you're going to need some of it to invest. (See Chapter 11.)

When you know what monthly payment you can afford and how much you can put down, when you have a good idea of the physical shape of the home you want, when you know whether you want to move far away or stay near, when you come to grips with the kind of lifestyle you'd prefer in your housing choice, when you've considered all the alternatives, then you're finally ready to make your $100,000 decision.

---

‡To find the after-tax value of other real estate, check with your accountant. Robert Irwin and Richard Brickman, *The Real Estate Agent's and Investor's Tax Book*, McGraw-Hill, 1980, is a good self-help source.

INDEX

INDEX